BUSES
YEARBOOK 2008
Edited by STEWART J. BROWN

Ian Allan
PUBLISHING

BUSES
YEARBOOK 2008

Contents

First published 2007

ISBN (10) 0 7110 3213 0
ISBN (13) 978 0 7110 3213 2

© Ian Allan Publishing Ltd 2007

Published by Ian Allan Publishing

an imprint of Ian Allan Publishing Ltd, Hersham, Surrey, KT12 4RG.
Printed in England by Ian Allan Printing Ltd, Hersham, Surrey, KT12 4RG.

Code: 0708/E1

Visit the Ian Allan Publishing website at
www.ianallanpublishing.com

Front cover:
It is now 10 years since the low-floor double-decker first appeared in the UK. The Alexander Dennis Enviro400 is based on the Dennis Trident chassis and has already won substantial orders. Stagecoach has standardised on the type, this example operating for its East Kent subsidiary. Mark Lyons

Back cover (upper):
The Scania/East Lancs Omnidekka has been a solid competitor to Dennis and Volvo products. This example is seen working for First Edinburgh. Gavin Booth

Back cover (lower):
Although the type is steadily disappearing, the MCW Metrobus remains in service in large numbers with Travel West Midlands, including this bus with the Travel Coventry operation. David Cole

Title page:
Step-entrance single-deckers are starting to become thin on the ground. This Plaxton Verde-bodied Scania N113CRB, new to Cardiff Bus, was part of the Lincolnshire Road Car fleet taken over by Stagecoach in 2005. Stewart J. Brown

Buses built in ...
where?

Things aren't always what they seem in the world of bus and coach manufacturing. ALAN MILLAR, Editor of Buses magazine, explores why vehicles which might appear to be Swedish or German could in fact be coming from Poland or Turkey.

Back in the summer of 1963 Coventry Corporation — a Labour-controlled council — accepted the lower of two tenders for the supply of its first 22 rear-engined double-deckers. Daimler, based in the city and the virtually exclusive supplier of its buses for many years, offered 22 Fleetlines for £149,000. But Leyland was prepared to let it buy 22 Atlanteans for £141,000.

Believe me, that was a lot of money then. Twenty-two new double-deckers today would cost an operator about £3.5 million; Leyland's price saved the council 5.4% in 1963, which at today's prices is over £180,000 and meant that it could obtain 22 Leylands for less than Daimler would charge for 21. While that may have conserved the council's precious funds, it was political dynamite. Shop stewards at Daimler protested at the export of work from Coventry to Lancashire, and while the council stuck to its guns and bought those Atlanteans, it didn't buy any more. All future purchases were of Coventry-built Fleetlines.

This was by no means unusual. Municipal operators often favoured their local manufacturers, even when the nearest alternative was perhaps only 100 or 200 miles and no more than two or three counties away. When everyone bought British, their loyalty was often to the chassis or bodybuilder nearest their doorstep, even if a competitor offered a superior product.

Compare that with just one example from much more recent times. Metro, the West Yorkshire PTE and a body answerable to councillors whose predecessors once made locally loyal purchasing decisions for the bus undertaking of Leeds, if not for Bradford, Huddersfield, Halifax or Todmorden, secured several million pounds of government funding for more than 150 yellow low-floor school buses. Having weighed up the options, Metro chose to buy the entire fleet from BMC in Turkey, even though another deal on offer would have given it a fleet of Optare Solos built in Leeds.

I can tell you that this decision went down as well at Optare — and at other British bus manufacturers — as Coventry's decision did with the Daimler shop stewards

over 40 years earlier, but Metro stuck by its decision, and BMC ended 2006 with around 3% of the year's market for new buses and coaches. It might also interest you to know that the 'B' in BMC once stood for 'British', as in the British Motor Corporation, which set the business up to assemble vehicles for the Turkish market. That connection has gone, and this BMC — BMC Sanayi, to use its full name — has long been a Turkish company building buses and trucks for domestic consumption and export — rather as the old BMC and other British manufacturers used to do in Britain.

This may be one of the more extreme examples of how the world of bus building and buying has changed within many of our lifetimes, but it is indicative of a wider trend. Purchasers feel much less bound by local or even national loyalties, and, increasingly, buses are being built in more distant countries with lower labour costs, for significantly less than previously. Nor is this a peculiarly British phenomenon. The same trend is evident across Western Europe, where bus buying is going through a similar process of change. And it's not just leading to the purchase of buses from new manufacturers like BMC. Big brands that you might once have taken for granted as being solidly Swedish or German conceal increasing numbers of vehicles produced in other countries you might imagine to be less industrially developed.

Ikarus flies in from Hungary

The biggest new sources of buses and coaches in the UK are Turkey, Poland and Hungary, with significant numbers part-built in Egypt and others potentially on their way from China, which in theory could meet the entire UK requirement in about one working week. The Indian bus-building industry also is upping its game. It's a process that began around 20 years ago and was perceived as a threat from the outset.

By the mid-1980s coach operators, in particular, were buying increasing proportions of their fleets from foreign factories, mainly in near Europe, Scandinavia and Portugal — more for the perceived reliability and

Above: A Turkish-built BMC Condor 220 owned by Metro and operated by First West Yorkshire. Alan Millar

technical superiority of those products than for their price. But at the same time a clear segment of the new-car market was being served by cheap imports from Central and Eastern Europe. They may have been the butt of many comedians' jokes, but the Russian Lada, the Czech Skoda, Polish Polski Fiat, Yugoslavian Yugo or Romanian Dacia appealed to motorists prepared to pay a lot less for recycled Western European technology put together in command economies where labour was cheap. Many small traders bought the van equivalents. Maybe there was room for their equivalents in the bus or coach markets. Indeed, briefly one was satisfied by coaches from Yugoslavia until that country tore itself apart in a series of civil wars.

Remember that the UK bus market was in turmoil. New Bus Grant had finally ended in 1984, forcing bus operators to pay the full price for their new vehicles for the first time in 16 years. At its peak, New Bus Grant paid half the price of every new vehicle operated on local routes, and there was a widely held view that it had helped inflate the cost of new buses. It certainly preserved more manufacturing capacity than a strictly commercial market could support, and operators took advantage of its final years to stock up with subsidised buses while they could.

Deregulation, in October 1986, added to the uncertainty. Routes were opened up to on-street competition, and local authorities invited competitive tenders for unremunerative routes, with the implication that the cheapest bids would usually win. Here was an opportunity for coach operators to enter a bus market previously in the grip of the public sector. And on top of all that, starting with the state-owned National Bus Company, the operating industry was to be privatised.

There was good reason to believe that old bus purchasing loyalties would be broken and that there would be a niche — conceivably quite a big one — for cheaper products imported from the sorts of places that provided budget-conscious motorists with rehashed 1960s Fiats.

The most obvious of these was Hungary, bus builder to the Soviet Bloc. Ikarus, in partnership with fellow Hungarian manufacturers Csepel (chassis, steering and gearboxes) and Raba (engines and axles), built up to 14,000 underfloor-engined buses and coaches a year, more than half of them for the Soviet Union in one of the complex barter deals that bound these countries together in a state of dependency. It wasn't the only bus manufacturer behind the Iron Curtain, but it was the biggest. It also exported buses to sympathetic states around the world and, as an expert in its field, secured some sales in countries that recognised virtues in its products — like Canada and the United States.

In the UK David Matthews's Kirkby group saw potential for Ikarus. Matthews had a vision for a new force in the bus- and coach-supply market and reasoned that a privatised industry would be less willing to be tied to traditional suppliers than it had been in the public sector. He talked of importing Ikarus buses incomplete and fitting them out in the UK, but when he did do a deal with Ikarus it was to import its Blue Danube coach body on Volvo B10M chassis. That was in 1987, but Kirkby looked to the much nearer East when it bought Plaxton the same year and changed its focus to protecting the UK's largest coach manufacturer from foreign competition.

That wasn't the end of the Ikarus story, however, as the Hungarians entered into a new relationship with Hughes DAF — the dealership owned by Cowie, which later became Arriva — to body the DAF SB220 bus for the UK from 1990 and later also to body the SB3000 coach with a product similar to the Blue Danube; MAN would also have a few bus bodies built on 18.220 chassis for the British Isles.

The Soviet Bloc had begun to collapse in 1989, and Ikarus would have a difficult — ultimately almost impossible — future as its once guaranteed 'home' market evaporated and it struggled to find new markets around the world. On the other hand, it possessed substantial technical expertise, and many of the major European bus builders expressed interest in acquiring it, either to give them access to the former Soviet Bloc markets or to provide them with a skilled low-cost manufacturing base (and ideally both). Rescue seemed at hand in 1999 when Irisbus — then owned jointly by Iveco and Renault — acquired a controlling interest. Unfortunately for the new owners Ikarus was competing in a fast-changing market. Other major Western European manufacturers were already making their own moves into these markets — several of them with factories we will meet a little later in this story — and were gaining sales at Ikarus's expense. Russia's own bus-manufacturing industry was consolidating, making Ikarus's biggest customer base less willing to purchase Hungarian buses, especially following the imposition of import duties.

And in any case, Irisbus already had a central European bus plant. In 1993 Renault had acquired a shareholding in Karosa, the Czech bus builder, and invested heavily in it, eventually using it to build school buses for the French market as well as continuing to supply its traditional customers. The successful

Below: An Ikarus E94-bodied MAN 18.220 operating in Dublin with Morton's of Rathfarnham. Eamon McArthur

Above: **Optare originally sourced bodies for its Alero minibus from NABI in Hungary. This later example operates in Nottingham on a feeder service to the city's main bus network.** Optare

transformation of the Czech factory into an integral part of Irisbus made the Ikarus development much less necessary, and in 2003 it axed the larger of its two remaining Hungarian factories, selling what was left back to Hungarian owners at the beginning of 2006.

As it began its slow disintegration, Ikarus had other impacts on the UK market. One of its factories was taken over by NABI — North American Bus Industries — in which Ikarus held a minority interest until 1997. This took up where Ikarus left off in the United States and supplied that tender-driven market with body shells, which were completed and fitted with drivelines in a factory in Alabama. NABI, which despite its name was Hungarian-owned, also targeted its home market, and as part of an ambitious expansion plan it bought Optare, the UK bus manufacturer, in January 2000. The relationship enabled Optare to sell its Solo midibus through the NABI network in the US and to source body shells for the Alero minibus from a NABI plant in Hungary. NABI also offered the Excel large low-floor single-decker in Hungary and built a version of its body on a step-entrance Scania chassis for that market. NABI eventually ran into financial trouble, closed its Hungarian plant, sold Optare back to its

management in 2005 and was itself taken over by American investors a few months later.

The other significant impact arose from the collapse of Csepel. As its sales volumes plummeted Ikarus had taken chassis-frame production in-house, leaving Csepel to try and develop markets of its own. Neoplan imported a couple of low-floor buses to the UK in 1997 on Csepel chassis with Cummins C-series engines, but the business closed two years later. However, a few of its key people found an unlikely new home — still in Budapest — with the British-owned Henlys group.

Henlys by then owned Plaxton, most of whose Pointer bodies went on Dennis Dart chassis. Henlys and Dennis thought they had agreed a friendly merger in 1998 until Mayflower — which owned Alexander — stepped in with an offer that was too big for Dennis's shareholders to ignore. With Mayflower keen to body as many Darts as it could Plaxton faced potential disaster in the bus market and used the ex-Csepel people as a short cut to match Mayflower's chassis-building capability. Along with other engineers recruited in the UK the Budapest people began developing a range of chassis that Henlys — which also owned Blue Bird in the US — could sell on either side of the Atlantic.

Two years later Henlys and Mayflower formed TransBus to amalgamate their interests, and although the Budapest team was retained and given other projects to pursue, the need for a Hungarian Dart

Right: The Plaxton Primo production line in Scarborough. The running units and body frame are built in Hungary.
Stewart J. Brown

clone was removed. After TransBus collapsed in 2004 — partly as a result of Mayflower's paying too much for Dennis — the business split in two and was rationalised. Alexander Dennis didn't need the Budapest office, but a nucleus of its people bought it and formed a new Anglo-Hungarian company, Enterprise Bus, to take up where Csepel and Henlys had left off. Their first project was a midibus, the Plasma, which it offered to build on behalf of partners around the world.

One of those partners is Plaxton, which re-entered the bus market after emerging from the TransBus wreckage, and which calls its version of the Plasma the Primo. Enterprise Bus, which has a design office in Lancashire and a small factory in Budapest, assembles the body frame and running units in Hungary and supplies that to Plaxton for glazing, panelling and fitting-out in Scarborough. If you study tax discs or read PSV Circle news-sheets you'll know that this is an Enterprise Bus vehicle, but as far as UK customers are concerned it's a Plaxton. The Plasma has also been supplied in left-hand-drive form to Hungarian customers, and Enterprise Bus wants to sell it through Designline in New Zealand.

Scandinavians take the Polish route
The modern Polish bus industry has also grown out of the collapse of the Soviet Bloc. Under the old regime two manufacturers built buses in the country. Autosan,

based in Sanok, produced a range of coaches and buses, while Wroclaw-based Jelcz built buses, most of them based on the Renault PR110 and powered by a licence-built Leyland 680 engine.

Post-1989 the major Western European manufacturers began to recognise the opportunities presented in Central and Eastern Europe, both as an enlarged market in which they could sell modern buses and also as a region in which they could build buses for local and wider consumption. As finance permitted, cities across the old Bloc began buying second-hand buses from Western European operators. Scandinavian, German, Dutch and French buses especially were shipped for new lives (often still in their previous owners' liveries), helping to create a customer base for new vehicles and an aftermarket for spare parts.

The two Swedish giants, Scania and Volvo, rode on this tide of westernisation, following the export of mid-life Danish and Swedish city and inter-urban buses with small-scale manufacture of their own products in joint ventures with Polish manufacturers. Scania set up a joint venture with a company called Kapena, based in the northern city of Slupsk, which previously repaired and reconditioned buses, and it later acquired control of the factory.

Like the other volume European bus manufacturers the two Swedish companies regard the passenger-transport market as a useful adjunct to their much larger truck-manufacturing businesses. It provides additional volume sales of engines and other major components, but it isn't always profitable. One way they can achieve profitability is to build bigger volumes of buses and coaches at lower cost; another is to build complete vehicles with body and chassis, rather than sacrificing some profit margin to an independent bodybuilding partner. Both already built complete buses in Scandinavia as a result of acquisitions of bodybuilders. Scania had acquired a company called SKV from Swedish Railways in 1966 and three years later moved its bus production from Södertälje, near Stockholm, to the SKV plant at Katrineholm, about 60 miles away. But, with the bus side of the business losing money, that began to change in 2001. First it moved chassis production back to Södertälje; then, during 2002, it moved truck production out of Slupsk to increase bus production there for sale across Europe, the process being completed in 2003 with the announcement of the impending transfer of all bus production from Sweden.

The most telling statement about the move was that labour rates in Sweden were five times those in Poland, yet build quality was comparable. In Sweden

this was not just because of higher wages but also because of the country's generous social-welfare system. In Poland, not only were labour rates lower, but the old regime's commitment to training and education created a skilled labour force — factors that would become apparent in the UK after Poland joined the European Union and huge numbers of young educated Poles emigrated in search of a better life. Scania also has a plant in Estonia, which supplies Scandinavia as well as its local market, and another in St Petersburg, which supplies Russia.

Volvo — exposed to the same cost factors — followed a similar path by a different route. Initially it set up a joint venture with Jelcz, primarily to assemble articulated B10Ms for the Polish market, but this fell apart and Jelcz became part of the EvoBus (Mercedes-Benz) importer's business, while Volvo set up on its own in Wroclaw. This began in 1995 as a joint venture with Finnish bodybuilder Carrus, which Volvo acquired three years later, prompting Volvo to turn the Polish plant into its production centre for complete buses and coaches for Central, Southern and Eastern Europe. This was part of a plant-rationalisation programme that ended Volvo bus-chassis production in the UK — at the former Ailsa plant in Irvine — as well as ultimately at some other body plants in Scandinavia, Austria and Germany.

Below: One of the first Polish-built Volvo 9700 coaches for the UK. The body design was built first by Carrus in Finland. Volvo

Above: A Scania OmniCity double-decker, the model built in Poland for the UK market, alongside the first Scania/MCW Metropolitan built for London Transport, with Swedish running units in a Birmingham-built body.
Alan Millar

Most UK production transferred to Sweden, but the tri-axle B10TL Super Olympian low-floor chassis for Hong Kong and Singapore transferred to Poland, as this was a relatively low-volume product. More recently Volvo has also begun selling the Wroclaw-built 9700 coach (a Carrus-bodied B12B, if you want this explained in cruder terms) in the UK, where it is pitched at the top end of the market.

Scania's Slupsk factory supplies the UK with the OmniCity and OmniLink single-deck buses and the OmniCity double-decker. It doesn't build coaches, as Scania's principal partner in many global coach markets is Irizar in Spain.

MAN also builds in Poland, but not yet for the UK market. Nor — yet — does the child of another German manufacturer's Polish venture. Neoplan, since acquired by MAN, set up a licensee outside Poznan to build buses and coaches for the Polish market. It was called Neoplan Polska, and the business was developed on an initial assumption that Neoplan would eventually own it. Instead, they went their separate ways in 2002, Neoplan Polska being renamed Solaris. It has expanded considerably, notably winning orders from Berlin and other German fleets, Switzerland, Scandinavia and France, as well as establishing itself as a source of affordable low-floor trolleybuses across Europe. The Solaris Trollino trolley can be found in Rome and Sweden as well as in several former Soviet Bloc states where trolleybuses play a big part in city transport systems. Significantly, when it won its first major order from Berlin, the city transport authority said it could also have bought MAN and Mercedes-Benz buses built in Turkey; the difference, apparently, was that German manufacturers didn't pass on the production cost savings, whereas Solaris did.

Although Solaris built two right-hand-drive low-floor buses for Malta it has yet to develop any products for the UK or Irish markets and maybe never will. But Autosan — now in common Polish ownership with Jelcz — has. It has tied up with Auto Holdings, which also sells Turkish BMCs in the British Isles, initially selling its Cummins-engined A1012 Eagle 12m rear-engined coach in Britain and Ireland. This is a low-cost basic vehicle in the mould of the old dual-purpose single-decker or could even be seen as a modern-day successor to something like a Duple Dominant-bodied Ford R-series. Sold here from 2004, it is offered both as a school bus or (particularly in Ireland) as a 55-seat short-haul private-hire coach. Auto Holdings is also considering selling Jelcz products (perhaps badged as Autosan, as that is easier for English speakers to pronounce) and in 2006 exhibited a low-floor midibus at the Euro Bus Expo show.

Turkey plucks its opportunity

The Soviet collapse may have played a small part in the growth of the Turkish bus-manufacturing industry. Before the two Germanys were unified in 1990 West Germany had an agreement with Turkey for its citizens to be employed in its factories as 'guest workers', providing a cheaper source of labour that later became available within its own boundaries when East Germany was absorbed. The same process also saw

Above: Articulated Solaris Urbino18s being delivered to BVG, the Berlin transport undertaking. Solaris

Below: An Autosan Eagle A1012T school bus with Rennie's of Dunfermline. David Love

the former Soviet republics of Turkmenistan and Uzbekistan import Turkish-built products — buses included — when the Iron Curtain was lifted.

These were only part of a bigger process of industrialisation of a country in which buses provide most public transport, which discourages imports and which is well placed to export to Middle Eastern markets as well as across Europe. It has been building up a domestic motor-manufacturing industry over the past 35 years, in part through collaboration with major Western European manufacturers.

The BMC Sanayi story is one of the lost opportunities that saddens those who remember a once glorious British-owned automotive industry, as well as being a clear example of how the world of vehicle manufacturing has changed. As recently as 1968 Leyland and bodybuilding partner Metro-Cammell Weymann supplied Istanbul, the principal Turkish city, with 300 Olympic single-deckers shipped out complete from Birmingham. Actually they were called Leyland Levends, because Olympic implied a Greek connection that would have gone down even worse than selling a Crossley Mancunian in Liverpool. But the point was that, 40 years ago, a big Turkish customer was buying complete vehicles from England.

The British Motor Corporation, which in 1968 became part of the brave new British Leyland, also sold trucks to Turkey and in 1964 had set up BMC Sanayi to assemble vehicles — buses, tractors and vans as well, eventually — under licence. British Leyland held a 26% shareholding in the company, but while its German competitors developed their Turkish partnerships Leyland pulled out in the early 1980s as — like a struggling octopus with a propensity to self-harm — it severed limb after limb in a quest for survival at home.

BMC Sanayi then forged a short-lived and none-too-successful technical partnership with Volvo but in 1986 became part of Cukurova, a major Turkish industrial group that set it on its continuing course of expansion. It turned to Breda, the Italian bus and train manufacturer, for integral-body technology and to American-owned manufacturers Cummins and Eaton for engines and axles respectively. Later it also acquired some body designs from Ikarus, while the truck-manufacturing side of the business supplied British manufacturer ERF with vehicles towards the end of its existence.

BMC's first move into the UK bus market came in 2001 in partnership with Marshall Bus, the Cambridge bodybuilder. At the Coach & Bus show that October it showed prototypes of two Turkish-built right-hand-drive bodied single-deckers that Marshall would complete and sell as part of its range. One was the 220SLF, a low-entry 12m 43-seater, while the other was the

1100FE 60-seat yellow school bus, targeted at a new market that FirstGroup was trying to create, initially with American-built Blue Birds. Alongside was the 850LLF, an 8.7m transverse-engined midibus chassis that Marshall had designed but planned to have BMC build for it in Turkey.

Before this relationship got much farther, Marshall Bus went bust. The Marshall group, which had been in and out of bus bodybuilding twice over the previous 40 years, had sold this side of the business to a management team that was backed by Slovakian investors. While this wasn't the end of either the BMC or the Marshall story, they went their separate ways.

BMC instead signed up with Auto Holdings, which has gradually built up a range of niche-market products at what it will readily admit is the cheaper end of the market. The 850LLF appears to have vanished without trace, and although a 220SLF appeared briefly on courtesy shuttle work at Gatwick Airport it was with other models that the marque began to establish itself in the UK and Ireland. Thanks to orders from First and Metro (and later also from Bus Éireann) the 1100FE has established a place for itself among customers seeking a modern-day equivalent of a Ford R-series to work during school term time. The rear-engined 850 Probus midicoach, with styling apparently derived from Ikarus, competes in the small sector seeking 35-seaters for longer-distance work.

BMC's big breakthrough with service buses came on the back of the Maltese government's decision to subsidise the modernisation of the island's bus fleet — most of which was second-hand, heavily rebuilt and, in many cases, almost unbelievably ancient — by contributing towards the purchase of a fleet of new 11m-long low-floor vehicles. The terms of the deal dictated buses cheaper than those being supplied new in the UK. The biggest proportion of new buses came from China, while BMC supplied the next-biggest, with a new rear-engined vehicle known as the Falcon 1100. Inside, by accident or design, this resembled the Marshall- and Park Royal-bodied ex-London Transport AEC Swifts still running on Malta. Outside it was adorned with a BMC badge with a definite Marshall look about it.

Auto Holdings identified a potential UK market for the 1100, target customers being those that habitually bought second-hand but would buy new if the price was right and those that considered the likes of new Dennis Darts and Optare Excels more expensive than they ought to be. Quite a few fetched up in fleets in rural Wales and Lincolnshire, while Chester City Transport took eight for new park-and-ride contracts at the end of 2003.

Falcon sales have tailed off, but BMC introduced the Ikarus-styled Hawk midibus in 2005, when it also

Right: A BMC 1100FE school bus operating in Co Cork with Ballincollig Coaches. Stephen Lynch

Left: Stagecoach Wales inherited six BMC Falcon 1100s with its acquisition in 2006 of the Glyn Williams fleet. Ben Morroll

Right: An MCV Evolution-bodied Dennis Dart for Docklands Buses on the bodybuilder's stand at Euro Bus Expo in November 2006. Chassis construction and body fittings and glazing are undertaken in England, the body framing being built in Egypt. Alan Millar

began supplying more than 150 Condor low-entry school buses to Metro, which allocates them to First and other contractors in West Yorkshire. The Condor is a reborn 220SLF, fitted out to a somewhat forbidding high-capacity layout specified by the customer. A conventionally seated service-bus version was launched in November 2006, when a prototype front-engined Nifty midicoach was also unveiled for possible later launch in the UK.

The Marshall bodybuilding business, meantime, reappeared as MCV Bus & Coach with a small factory near Ely in the Cambridgeshire fens. It had a difficult birth, as Marshall bodied the Dennis Dart, but TransBus — trying to protect its own bodybuilding capacity — refused to supply the new business with chassis. After building an initial batch of Darts for Warrington (which had ordered them from Marshall) it had to look elsewhere and eventually established a partnership with MAN to body its 14.220 and 12.220 chassis.

Such a setback could have sunk a conventional business, but MCV's overseas connections helped save it. Most outsiders assumed — and its UK management did nothing to discourage the assumption — that MCV was some sort of abbreviation that at least implied a connection with Marshall. After all, it had acquired the rights to the Marshall body range, which had begun life as the Duple Dartline body on the original Dart, and it began by pursuing the Marshall customer base. It emerged later that it was, in fact, related to MCV, a high-volume bodybuilder producing mainly Mercedes-Benz-based buses and coaches in Egypt. It builds the body frames on to right-hand-drive chassis in Egypt and ships them to Cambridgeshire for fitting out. This arrangement says much about the economics of 21st-century bus building, as Alexander Dennis does what TransBus wouldn't do and supplies MCV with Dart chassis to complement its MAN range. Those chassis are built in Guildford, shipped out to Egypt, bodied up to the framework stage, then shipped back to England for completion.

Temsa, Mercedes and MAN

The other Turkish-owned manufacturer selling into the UK is Temsa. It began life in 1984 importing Mitsubishi products from Japan and started building a 12m Mitsubishi-designed coach three years later. It subsequently developed its own range of coaches, from midicoach to 14m tri-axle, using MAN and DAF engines, ZF gearboxes and axles and secured the services of Bob Lee, the Swiss-born former Managing Director of Neoplan, to provide it with some of the design and engineering credibility it needed to break into Western Europe. It also signed up Wim Van Hool, of the Belgian coachbuilding family, to develop a mainstream European sales organisation.

While BMC is firmly in the cheap, cheerful and basic end of the market, Temsa aims to achieve mainstream European style and quality levels at a competitive price. Its biggest European success so far has been achieved in France, where it has sold more than 1,000 vehicles, many of them school-cum-inter-urban buses. It also has done rather well in the much smaller Austrian market, securing substantial repeat orders from the state-owned Postbus company. In the UK it sells two products — the 12m Safari and the Opalin midicoach — through Arriva Bus & Coach, the former Hughes DAF, which regards the Safari as spiritual successor to the Ikarus-bodied DAF SB3000.

For a hint of what might otherwise have become of the BMC/Leyland partnership one need look no farther than Mercedes-Benz and MAN. Mercedes held a minority shareholding in a company called Otomarsan, which from 1967 built some of its bus and coach products in Istanbul. In 1990 it increased its shareholding to 62%, renaming the company Mercedes-Benz Türk, and five years later opened a new factory 30 miles away at Hosdere. This has become an integral part of the Mercedes global plan, building vehicles for export to the former Soviet Bloc and for a growing number of Western European countries. The O345 Conecto bus, for example, can be found in Russia, Latvia, France (as a rural school bus), Germany and Belgium. In 1998 it launched the left-hand-drive O350 Tourismo coach into mainstream European markets and in 2006 began selling the updated right-hand-drive version in the UK and Ireland. Until then its principal UK coach was the Touro, with a chassis bodied under contract in Portugal in a joint venture with Caetano.

MAN doesn't sell Turkish-built products in the UK, but Tourliner coaches built by its Neoplan subsidiary do come from there. It initially had a 33% shareholding in MANAS, a joint venture set up in 1966 with its importer, which had been selling MAN products in Turkey since 1950. It has built up its financial stake in stages since then, reaching 93% in 1998, the Turkish plant supplying MAN-badged vehicles into Germany, France and more price-conscious global markets.

China and India

For now the bus-manufacturing industries of China and India are focused most closely on meeting growing demand for large numbers of modern vehicles. Volvo, to name but one of the big players, is involved in joint ventures in both countries, selling recognisably European vehicles with models barely different from those sold in the UK or mainland Europe.

This may change, however, as manufacturers in those countries also offer acceptable products, at significantly lower cost, in Europe. Chinese-built

Right: One of the first Turkish-built Mercedes-Benz Tourismo coaches for the UK. Alan Millar

Left: A Turkish-built Mercedes-Benz Conecto in Riga, the capital of Latvia. Keith Shum

Right: The Neoplan Tourliner coach, introduced in the UK in 2006, is built in Turkey. Alan Millar

coaches can be found, for example, in Cyprus, while the one Chinese manufacturer to sell so far into the UK has a Maltese connection. King Long developed the Cummins-engined XMQ6113 low-entry bus for the Maltese fleet-renewal programme and went on to sign up with Auto Holdings to sell buses and coaches alongside its Turkish and Polish products, which also have Cummins engines.

As I write this in early 2007 the one bus built for demonstration in the UK had entered service (alongside some BMC Falcon 1100s) a few months earlier with McKindless of Wishaw, a large Scottish independent that until then had bought only second-hand. For coach customers Auto Holdings offered the XMQ6127, also with Cummins engine (the 11-litre ISMe, which is still rare in UK coaches) and an odd amalgam of various different European manufacturers' styling touches. It planned initially to sell it as a comprehensively equipped luxury coach for a fraction of the price of a European one, but before getting any into service had changed its tack to talk instead of pitching it at the more basic end of the market. While King Long has still to make its presence felt, it may yet do so.

Chinese manufacturers also were circling, apparently prepared to buy TransBus if the Plaxton and Alexander Dennis rescue bids had not succeeded instead.

As yet there are no Indian vehicles in the UK, but one of the big Indian manufacturers shows every capability of changing that one day. In 2005 Tata (whose parent company acquired Corus, which incorporates what used to be British Steel, at the beginning of 2007) acquired a minority shareholding in Spanish bodybuilder Hispano, which sells small numbers of coaches in the UK and Ireland. The logic of the deal was that Hispano required the capital available from Indian finance, while Tata required the technical expertise on offer from Spain.

With British companies already exporting thousands of call-centre and back-office accounting jobs to India it is entirely conceivable that some of our buses or coaches could also be sourced from the Asian sub-continent in a few years from now. It may sound far-fetched today, but the bus world has already changed immensely since Coventry ordered those Atlanteans from seemingly far-off Lancashire.

Below: The only Chinese-built King Long sold so far for local bus operation in the UK entered service with McKindless towards the end of 2006. Gary Mitchelhill

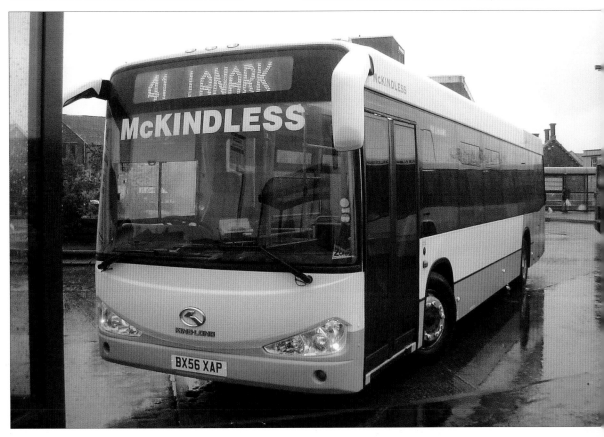

Route branding around Britain

Colourful branding has become widespread as a way of raising the profile of selected bus services. TONY WILSON illustrates a selection of branded routes from around the country.

Like it or not, boldly branded buses are on the increase and are here to stay. And in recent years branding has developed quite dramatically, in many cases being applied as an all-over livery, rather than being restricted to a listing of place names on the side of the vehicle.

While I approve of route branding, I am quite aware that there are those who do not, and, of course, problems can occur, in particular allocating a branded bus to the wrong route.

It is tempting to think of route branding as something new, but this form of promotion has been around for longer than many people think. Whilst it may not have evolved with the invention of the wheel, route branding, like advertising, has adorned the sides of buses since the time of the horse-drawn vehicle. From early days, when there were very few such services, route details

were visible on the sides of vehicles either in the form of slip-boards or applied with paint directly onto the bodywork.

Nowadays it is vinyl that dominates, even the windows being used to extol the virtues of some services, which is not a good thing. Windows are for looking out of.

In some areas branding comprises bold all-over liveries used to differentiate routes within networks. Go to Newcastle or Nottingham, for example, to be faced with almost all the colours of the rainbow as operators entice custom with their gaily painted buses.

The pictures which follow, arranged in a clockwise fashion around the British mainland, starting and ending in Scotland, provide a flavour of how this medium has been applied and used to promote various services.

Left: In July 1990 the Fife Scottish name was still around, as indeed was this Alexander-bodied Volvo B10M double-decker. One does not necessarily link the colour grey with smart, but on this occasion it worked well with the contrasting red and the branding that had been applied. Marketed as the 'Fife Coastliner', route 57 ran from Edinburgh across the Forth road bridge and then hugged the southern coast of Fife all the way to Leven.

Right: There can be little doubt as to the route to which this Go North East bus is assigned. Having vinyl plastered over the windows must be somewhat frustrating for passengers as it hinders the view, in this case both front and either side of this Wright Eclipse Gemini-bodied Volvo B7TL. The X10 runs hourly between Newcastle and Middlesbrough via Stockton-on-Tees.

Below: Maintained at around 20 vehicles, the fleet of Blazefield Holdings subsidiary Yorkshire Coastliner, running a network of services linking Leeds with the coastal towns of Bridlington, Filey, Scarborough and Whitby, has always been a smart one. Route branding on vehicles assigned to the 840 group of routes covers all the major points served, as illustrated on this Wright-bodied Volvo B10B negotiating the steep descent from the North Yorkshire Moors into Goathland in April 2003.

Above: During a period of takeover and change and before the complete introduction of Arriva's corporate image in the North East of England some local liveries were still in evidence. The name Trimdon Motor Services is recalled by the livery (along with letters and crest below the driver's window) on this DAF/Optare Delta at the top end of Stockton High Street in August 1998. Several buses were dedicated to route 16, marketed as 'The Stockton-Thornaby Connection'.

Below: As the era of the National Bus Company was drawing to a close East Midland Motor Services introduced a service between Lincoln and Manchester, marketed as the Lincman. During the course of its journey of almost 100 miles the X67 served Newark, Mansfield and Chesterfield, where an Alexander TE-bodied Leyland Tiger is seen pulling away from the bus station.

Above: Long before Mercedes-Benz, Scania or Volvo introduced today's versions of the articulated single-decker examples of the Leyland-DAB were serving the inhabitants of Sheffield. Originally operated by South Yorkshire Transport, the bus fleet was subsequently acquired by FirstGroup, including the artics, some of which were used on the service that linked the city centre with the edge-of-town shopping complex at Meadowhall. Several of these buses ran in the dedicated livery seen here in the city centre in May 1999.

Left: In 1999 East Midland, by now part of Stagecoach, was awarded the contract to operate the Virgin Trains Rail Link service between Macclesfield, on the West Coast main line, and Buxton. Certain journeys were extended to Chatsworth House; seen here in the vast parkland is one of three dedicated Dennis Super Pointer Darts fitted with extra luggage racks and dual-purpose seating.

Above: Rail-link services have become a popular extension to the nation's rail network. These are also quite varied in nature, ranging from some quite lengthy cross-country routes to urban services like this one linking the city centre and the railway station in Cambridge. Back in April 2000 it was in the hands of a small batch of Marshall-bodied Volvo B6 midibuses.

Right: When tenders were invited for London's Routemaster-operated route 19 from Battersea to Finsbury Park the successful bidder was Kentish Bus & Coach, a company that derived from London Country Bus Services. Gone was the traditional London red, replaced by Kentish Bus maroon and cream livery with route branding. In April 1993 a Routemaster pulls out of Hester Road, Battersea, the southern terminus of the route, and into Battersea Bridge Road, to take up service on a short working to Tottenham Court Road station.

Above: With the opening in November 1959 of the M1 motorway Midland Red took the opportunity to introduce its Motorway Express service between Birmingham and London, using a fleet of these handsome BMMO CM5T 37-seater coaches built in-house. At first 'Birmingham-London' route boards appeared above the windows, but as more services were introduced a revised branding was put in place.

Below: Midland Red's motorway services proved so successful that in 1965 higher-capacity coaches were introduced in the shape of the longer, 46-seat CM6T. Manœuvring in London's Victoria Coach Station, one shows off the route details inserted into sections cut out of the bodywork above the windows.

Right: Looking more like an all-over advertisement bus than anything else was this ECW-bodied Bristol LH operated by Wilts & Dorset in August 1987. Given that such advertising was much in vogue at the time one could have been excused for missing the point that the bus was dedicated to the Poole Quay Shuttle service to/from the railway station.

Left: Until recently the X53 route through Devon and Dorset was an infrequent service linking Exeter with Dorchester, a distance of 60-odd miles. Among the vehicles assigned to the route in the late 1990s was this Plaxton-bodied Volvo B10M coach operated by FirstGroup's Southern National subsidiary. Discreet route branding was applied beneath the windows.

Right: In 2004 the X53 route was upgraded in a number of ways. Marketed as the Jurassic Coast route, the service was revised east of Bridport to serve Weymouth, continuing thence to Poole and, on some journeys, Bournemouth. A new and much-improved timetable, extensive publicity and a fleet of new vehicles all contributed, and the enhanced service proved to be a great success, with passenger numbers growing year on year. Magnificent views of the coastline are afforded from the upper deck of the East Lancs-bodied Scania N94s that replaced the single-deckers used hitherto; this one is seen in Bridport in June 2004.

Above: In a number of areas Arriva's corporate livery of aquamarine and stone can be seen adorned with a standard type of branding, the locations served by the route in question being shown as bullet points on a thick red line. Pictured in Llandudno in May 2001 is a Plaxton Pointer-bodied Dennis Dart SLF on route 12 to Rhyl.

Below: In contrast, 10 years earlier a number of Stagecoach buses used on routes in the Lake District wore this pleasant pseudo-Southdown livery, which suited this area of outstanding natural beauty. In June 1996 a pristine ex-Southdown ECW-bodied Bristol VRT departs the southern terminus of route 79 at Seatoller.

Above: In 2006 the X35 route between Kendal and Barrow-in-Furness in Cumbria was upgraded by the introduction of a small fleet of East Lancs-bodied Dennis Tridents, one of which is seen swinging onto the forecourt of the railway station at Grange-over-Sands. A partnership between Stagecoach and Cumbria County Council is advertised, with bold route branding on the blue and green livery, possibly to illustrate a connection between the seaside and the mountainous Lake District.

Below: And so back to Edinburgh. Lothian Buses was the first customer for the double-deck version of the Polish-built Scania OmniCity, ordering an initial batch of five for its Airlink service between Waverley station and the airport, on the city's western fringe. One is seen in Princes Street in September 2006.

Terminal delights

Bus stations come in all shapes and sizes. MICHAEL H. C. BAKER looks back at bus stations he has known, from Shenzhen to Sussex.

All photographs by the author or from the author's collection

It has to be said that, unlike the great Victorian railway stations, most bus stations can hardly lay claim to any great architectural merit. There are a few exceptions, including — pleasing to note — some recent ones, but on the whole bus stations are pretty utilitarian affairs. (Indeed, just what constitutes a bus station proper, as opposed to a bit of roadway with some markings painted on the surface, is in itself a discussion point.) However, what the average bus station lacks in style it makes up for in action, for there is usually something of note going on, and not just amongst the vehicles. All sorts of people congregate at bus stations, and not, generally — how shall I put it? — well, let us say, the young executive type. Indeed, I have never quite worked out why so many coach companies advertise 'executive travel' when I have always understood that once you had reached the dizzy heights of being an executive — I do not speak from personal experience, you understand — your aim was never again to travel by public transport.

My first experience of a bus station came in 1940 at Bognor Regis, whither my parents and I had gone after having been bombed out of our home in Thornton Heath. Having rented a bungalow in Felpham, we would regularly travel by bus to the town centre and alight inside the bus station, which, although I didn't realise it at the time, was perhaps the finest example of an art-deco bus station in the country — not that it had a lot of rivals. Its glazed-tile frontage was a wonderful period piece, now sadly demolished, although a similar one at Eastbourne survives.

Like many bus stations these incorporated a garage, a feature which sometimes confuses the public and,

Below: A Southdown all-Leyland PD2 pulls out of the art-deco bus station in Bognor Regis in the summer of 1961.

indeed, the management. One often comes across notices warning passengers not to venture into the garage area of these establishments, which are blithely ignored for the very good reason that buses must sometimes be boarded there or that it provides a perfectly good right of way. Kingston-upon-Thames was a good example of this within the London Transport empire. It was possible to get a double-deck bus inside Kingston bus station, but the single-deckers made it quite clear that this was their territory — on my first visit these included assorted AECs — Ts, six-wheel LTs and side-engined Qs — as well as postwar Leyland Tiger TDs. All of which was quite an eye-opener to someone growing up in the totally double-deck world of Thornton Heath Pond.

Thornton Heath has never had a bus station proper. Ever since its tram depot was replaced by a garage (in 1952) buses have lined up on the generous forecourt, but never, to my knowledge, have passengers been allowed to board there. Croydon did scarcely any better. The nearest it got in the 1940s and '50s were stands beside West Croydon railway station, where a number of red and green bus routes and the 630 trolleybus terminated. Eventually a proper bus station was built on the site, and this also accommodates electric traction, Tramlink cars calling every few minutes.

I find much fascination in how they do things abroad. Having said that, fascination does not quite describe the feeling of my wife and I when we arrived at

Shenzhen on our first visit to China. Our son, William, and his wife, Jeed, were staying with relations there, and we, having flown in from the UK to Hong Kong, had been instructed to board a bus and alight at the bus station in Shenzhen, a city which adjoins Hong Kong, where they would meet us. This we duly did. However, there was no sign of them, and it dawned on us that we were in a vast, very foreign bus station, where our mobile phones did not work, and where we could read absolutely nothing, either on the notices all around or on the buses themselves, except for the occasional advertisement in English. We suddenly felt very far from home. Fortunately William and Jeed soon appeared, and all was well.

Thailand is another very foreign country, but one that has become gradually more familiar as we regularly visit our son and his family there. Its bus stations are in many ways a microcosm of the country itself, where one can watch the world going about its business, seemingly all of a bustle. Yet the locals are only too willing to help visitors, if it is obvious that help is required. There are three huge long-distance bus stations in Bangkok, and practically every town and village has a designated area for both local and long-distance buses, usually right beside the market in the town centre.

A setting beloved of Hollywood in its black-and-white days was the railway station, which in technicolour (sorry, 'color') days has rather been superseded by the bus station — usually far less grand, although sometimes they are one and the same; I can think of Trois Rivières in Canada, for example, where a splendid waiting room on the station platform was solely for the use of bus passengers, with the only trains passing through being freight ones.

In the same state as Hollywood, I once took a Greyhound bus from San Francisco to Sacramento. The Transbay terminal off Mission Street was nothing much to write home about, although it was perfectly adequate, and both passengers and vehicles were under cover. Across the other side of San Francisco Bay we picked up more passengers at Oakland, at a dark, gloomy bus station, not much in keeping with the views to the west, and then off we headed eastwards.

We had been warned of the peculiarities of the San Francisco climate and discovered exactly what these entailed when we alighted at our destination. The temperature when we boarded our bus had been around 64°F, and with a brisk wind blowing off the sea and heavy mist it felt cooler. In Sacramento it was 100°F. Which meant we had to lug around our redundant jumpers whilst we explored the delights of the state capital. These included what was modestly described as 'The World's Finest Railway Museum' (well, this *was* California), a sanitised replica of a Wild West town and a nice stern-wheel paddle-steamer which I watched head up the Sacramento River under the railway bridge, which had to be raised for its passage.

And so to Halifax. In deepest West Yorkshire they have one of the more recent and therefore better-designed bus stations with plenty of covered waiting areas, much of it with seating and clearly marked pedestrian crossings leading to the various stands. And the setting is spectacular enough in the heart of the Pennines.

For many years I used to bring a troop of nine-year-olds for a week's adventures in Yorkshire, and on several occasions our Wallace Arnold coach was driven by a former Halifax Corporation driver who owned an ex-Southdown Harrington-bodied Leopard — 'because I fell in love with them when they used to call into our coach station on their way to Scotland in the 1960s'. We would partake of a fish supper at the Blue Dahlia chippie (just around the corner from the bus station), run by a friendly proprietor and which gave the Dorset boys and girls a perfect introduction to Yorkshire cuisine, although they couldn't always fathom his accent and, sadly, used to exclaim 'Ugh!' at that wonderful delicacy of the district, mushy peas; we never dared offer them tripe.

Moving a little way east finds us in Bradford, with a good example of a transport interchange (opened in 1977) where the bus station is combined with a railway one. Somewhat unusually, the bus station is also entirely under cover. Densely populated West Yorkshire has, not surprisingly, a plethora of bus stations. I can't say I found Wakefield very impressive, although if you had a soft spot for the Lynx, as I did for Leyland's last full-size single-deck design, this was a good place to see examples of the species.

We have noted that bus stations are often, sensibly enough, located right beside railway stations. London's Victoria is perhaps the best known, with the coach station and also the Green Line facility close by. For several years in my student days I worked as a porter at the railway station, and I would sometimes convey passengers and their luggage between one establishment and the other. These were not, one soon realised when loaded down with several cases, as close to each other as one had supposed on other occasions when loaded only with camera and notebook. The coach station was a veritable Mecca for the enthusiast, particularly at the height of summer. We're talking about the early 1960s, when, as long as one was not too distracted by miniskirts, microskirts and the other delights of Swinging London (and Victoria is only five minutes' ride on a No 11 from Sloane Square and the King's Road, Chelsea), one could observe a wonderful variety of liveries and body styles, not only packed into Victoria Coach Station but overflowing into the nearby streets and elegant squares. Although the underfloor-engined coach had been with us for a decade there were still half-cabs to be seen working reliefs, and even the occasional prewar Maidstone & District Tiger (with postwar body), as well as Bedford/Duple OBs, often hired in from small, faraway businesses.

It was around this time that I found employment on Merseyside, at the art college in Southport to be precise, and I was intrigued to discover that the bus station was not so much close to the railway station as actually inside one. Lord Street station, which had been used by Cheshire Lines trains, had closed in the early 1950s, and Ribble, having acquired it for £72,000, reopened it as a bus station in the summer of 1954. Within I found dark-red Ribble Leyland PD3s, a design beloved of that company. Some were fitted with utilitarian Metro-Cammell bodies, others with a much more elegant, Blackpool-built Burlingham design. There were also PD2s and all-Leyland Royal Tigers, as well as cream-and-red AEC Regents and Leyland Titans of St Helens Corporation, wearing a livery very similar to that used by Southport, whose buses passed by in Lord Street but did not venture inside. In its reincarnated form it was a most impressive

Above: London's Victoria Coach Station in 1955, with three Maidstone & District coaches. Two are AEC Reliances, while the third, on the extreme right, is an AEC Regal.

Below: Victoria offered variety in liveries and body styles. Also seen in 1955 was this Windover-bodied Leyland Tiger PS1 of Southdown.

reincarnated form it was a most impressive establishment, almost certainly the only Victorian bus station, but sadly it never fulfilled its potential. Upon the division of Ribble in 1986 it passed to the new North Western company, which could not resist selling it off almost immediately, and it is now a shopping centre, although the façade remains.

Like railway stations in steam days, bus stations are not always conducive to a healthy existence, especially if they are under cover and the only outlets for exhaust fumes are at either end. In this respect that in Maidstone, underneath a multi-storey car park and shopping centre, was a particularly foul example. The town really ought to have known better, for it had plenty of experience, being home to England's first bus station, opened in 1922 by Maidstone & District. The company was a pioneer in this respect, throughout its territory setting up bus stations which, although more or less in the open air, could boast waiting rooms, ticket/booking offices and toilets. That at Hawkhurst, on the Kent/Sussex border, has always struck me as being unusually elaborate for what is quite a small town.

The original Maidstone establishment lasted until 1976. I knew it well in the 1950s, when it would be full of a fascinating mix of rebodied wartime Daimler double-deckers, very early postwar Bristols (a fairly unusual choice for a BET company, but one which M&D favoured), all-Leyland PD2s and prewar AEC Regents and Titans that had been rebuilt as coaches by the local firm of Beadle.

Maidstone's bus station was also served by East Kent, with rebodied prewar Titans and early postwar Guys. These ran on routes from Folkestone and Canterbury, their livery of deep cherry red providing an attractive contrast with the beautiful dark green and off-white (with silver roof) of Maidstone & District. The tables were turned at Canterbury, where red buses greatly outnumbered green at St Peter's Place bus station, within sight of the cathedral — well, what isn't in that modestly sized city? This was replaced long ago — the bus station, not the cathedral — by one the other side of the city but still within the walls.

Whilst to the east Maidstone & District met East Kent (and at one time would nearly amalgamate with it), to the west, all along the Kent/Sussex border and the Weald, it came into contact with Southdown. The latter had bus stations at Uckfield (down at the bottom of the town by the railway station), Heathfield, Lewes, and — best known of all — Pool Valley, in Brighton.

For those who consider the contrasting green-based liveries of M&D and Southdown among the finest of all time, Pool Valley was an æsthetic delight. I'm not sure it was quite so popular with passengers, who, after all, provide bus companies with rather more income than do enthusiasts. The problem was that, although it was on the seafront and only a few hundred yards from the Palace Pier, it was a fair distance from the main shopping district. This became even more of a problem when the Churchill Square complex opened, and

Above: Canterbury bus station in wartime, with East Kent Leylands and Dennises.

Below: Brighton's Pool Valley bus station, with assorted Southdown double-deckers and one from Maidstone & District. This is a 1960 view. Pool Valley remains in use as a coach station.

alighting points are to be found. It is certainly not a bus station, being merely a street with a line of bus stops and shelters on either side. Pool Valley nevertheless remains in use as a coach terminus.

In some towns and cities the profit to be made in selling off the site occupied by a bus station has been too tempting to resist, the pound signs flashing to the exclusion of passenger convenience and the need to encourage the use of public transport. However as the world, becomes ever more aware of the threat to the environment, public transport is seen very much as A Good Thing and therefore to be encouraged. This includes making it easier to travel in and out of the centre by bus or tram — so it seems a safe bet that customer-friendly boarding and alighting points will continue to be a feature of our towns and cities.

Above: The stylish bus station in Whitley Bay, with a Northumbria Leyland National, in 1995. Both bus and station have since gone.

Right: Penzance bus station looking bleak in November 2005, with two potential passengers, one seagull and a First London Olympian a long way from home.

Above: A warning for pedestrians at Bath bus station in 2006. The coach is one of a batch of 12.8m-long Plaxton-bodied Volvos which were used as a trial in the provision of space for passengers in wheelchairs. It has a wheelchair lift mounted within the wheelbase.

Below: A host of Wilts & Dorset buses, ranging from a 27-year-old Bristol VRT to a new Mercedes-Benz Citaro, jostle for position in Poole bus station in November 2006.

South-west 'Seventies

In the summer of 1976 photographer **GEOFF MILLS** spent time in the South West of England, recording the fast-changing scene.

Above: The only municipal bus fleet in the far South West was in Plymouth, where the Corporation had been an early convert to the high-capacity Leyland Atlantean. This example, with 77-seat Metro-Cammell body, was new in 1964 and typified deliveries to Plymouth in the period 1960-6.

Below: Plymouth was also quick to add Leyland Nationals to its fleet, taking 15 in 1972 and 30 in 1973. All were 11.3m-long dual-door 46-seaters.

Top: With the creation of the National Bus Company there were big changes in the South West involving the associated former Tilling Group Southern National and Western National companies, and the ex-BET Devon General business. BET had been a big user of the Atlantean, represented by this 1959 Devon General bus in Torquay in NBC poppy red.

Above: A batch of convertible open-top Atlanteans delivered to Devon General were named after great sailors, becoming known as 'Sea Dogs'. Commemorating arguably the most famous seafarer in English history, Sir Walter Raleigh leaves Torquay for Brixham. The bus had been new in 1961 and had a Metro-Cammell body.

Right: Devon General had used a dark-red livery, and this was still to be seen in 1976, albeit on a rapidly decreasing number of buses. A survivor was this AEC Regent V with 59-seat forward-entrance Willowbrook body, one of six identical buses delivered in 1965.

Left: Among the last new vehicles to be delivered in traditional Devon General livery was this 1971 AEC Reliance with Willowbrook body, one of a batch of 14. Note the low positioning of the fleetname to leave space for an advertisement on the side.

Right: Among the obvious early changes at Devon General was the arrival of new Bristol VRTs, in a double-deck fleet made up mainly of AEC Regents and Atlanteans. This 70-seater entered service in 1971 and originally carried the company's traditional colours, although by 1976 it was in poppy red.

Above: The Exeter Corporation fleet was acquired by NBC in 1970 and absorbed by Devon General. Most of Exeter's double-deckers were Leyland Titans; this Massey-bodied PD2A was one of five delivered in 1965 which were the undertaking's last new double-deckers.

Below: At the time of the sale of the Exeter bus fleet the Corporation had on order two batches of Leyland Panthers, totalling 14 in all, and these were delivered to Devon General in 1970 and 1971. Marshall built the 47-seat bodywork, of the briefly fashionable two-door layout designed to speed boarding and alighting on one-man-operated buses.

Above: A Bristol MW6G of Western National pauses in Barnstaple. It had started life in 1960 as a 39-seat coach but by 1976 had been fitted with 41 bus seats.

Below: Operators in Devon often bought small coaches for use on the region's narrow roads. One of the more unusual vehicles to carry NBC's corporate white coach livery was this Greenslades Bedford VAS5 with 7ft 6in-wide 29-seat Duple Dominant body — often called the 'Baby Dominant' in its guise as a small coach. New in 1974, it was operated until 1980.

Top: Western National ran examples of Bristol's smallest model, which in the 1960s had been the SU. These two vehicles in Totnes depot are SUL4A models, the '4A' indicating a four-cylinder Albion engine, which was the standard power for the model. On the left is a 33-seat coach from 1968, on the right a 36-seat bus from 1966; both have ECW bodies. The 1966 buses were among the last SUs built.

Above: With the end of SU production a few Tilling Group companies specified Bedford VAM chassis with ECW bodywork. Western National took 12 of these unusual buses in 1967.

Above: The LH was Bristol's last light-duty chassis. Most of those for NBC had ECW bus bodies, but a few were bodied as coaches. Among the more unusual coaches were 10 LH6Ls supplied to Royal Blue in 1973/4, which had 39-seat Marshall bodies. This one is in London, in the coach park at Battersea.

Below: A more typical LH loads in Bideford. Early ECW-bodied LHs — this is a 1969 bus — had flat windscreens. The bus is still in Tilling green and cream, albeit with corporate NBC fleetname on the cove panels.

Above:.The Bristol Lodekka was the standard double-decker in the Western and Southern National fleets in the 1950s and 1960s. This is a 1962 FLF6B in Truro.

Below: This stylish Alexander-bodied bus, seen in Plymouth's Bretonside bus station, is an unusual Leyland Atlantean PDR1/3 with drop-centre rear axle; most low-height Alexander bodies of this style were fitted to Daimler Fleetlines. One of five delivered to Western Welsh in 1971, it passed to Western National the following year.

Step Change

GAVIN BOOTH charts the journey from the Leyland National in the 1970s to low-floor single-deckers in the 1990s.

All photographs by Gavin Booth

For many British bus operators the Leyland National was the single-decker of the 1970s. But it's fair to say that it didn't win that accolade in some kind of countrywide vote; if it had, the voting papers from National Bus Company fleets would have listed just one candidate, the aforementioned Leyland National. And the cross would probably have been pre-printed on the form.

But that was how it was. For much of the 1970s the Leyland National was the only single-deck bus that NBC companies could buy, not necessarily because it was a great bus, but because NBC was a partner with Leyland in the brave new let's-build-a-standardised-single-deck-bus-in-a-new-factory project.

It would be unfair to suggest that the same applied to every bus operator in Britain. Some bought Nationals voluntarily, though in truth there wasn't much of a choice. Leyland had protected its investment in the National by discontinuing production of its rival products, so the AEC Swift/Merlin, Daimler Roadliner and Leyland Panther and Panther Cub were no longer available, and probably not greatly missed. What was

missed — and this was possibly a great miscalculation — was the Bristol RE. Within NBC the RE had been successfully doing what the new National would be expected to do — and more. In 1962 it had introduced to Britain a new kind of urban single-decker, with its engine at the rear and, consequently, a fairly low floor ahead of the rear axle. Not a stepless low floor as we now know it, but a considerably easier bus for passengers to use than the alternatives, which in 1962 were underfloor-engined models with unavoidably high floorlines and a climb of several steps to the interior.

So what was wrong with the RE? Essentially nothing — except it was there and could divert sales away from Leyland's new National. NBC companies, which had been the main RE customers anyway, were simply not allowed to buy the RE; the customers it had won in the municipal sector would have to look elsewhere.

Below: **Northern Ireland was regarded by Leyland as an export market to justify the continuing supply of Bristol REs to Ulsterbus and Citybus long after the model had ceased to be available in Britain. This is a 1984 RELL6G with Alexander body, in Belfast in 1996.**

Above: The Dennis Falcon HC was a Bristol RE substitute that sold mainly to municipal operators. This 1983 example with boxy East Lancs body was new to Ipswich but by 2000 had found its way via the Leicester Citybus fleet to First Leicester.

Except, of course, if you were in Northern Ireland, or indeed anywhere other than Britain. Ulsterbus made its feelings about the National very plain. It didn't want any, and it wanted REs instead. Leyland didn't want to lose the Ulsterbus business, and it certainly didn't want some pesky foreigner like Scania or Volvo getting a foothold there. The cunning plan was to designate Northern Ireland as an 'export' market and so continue to supply REs to Ulsterbus until 1984.

The absence of REs from the home market didn't deter other manufacturers from reinventing it, sometimes with a little nudging from operators that didn't care for Leyland's growing monopoly. Seddon tried with the RU, Dennis with the Falcon, and there was even the Ward GRX11. Only Darlington Transport bought the Ward, but the RU and Falcon found their customers, though hardly in sufficient numbers to worry Leyland too much.

What Leyland should probably have been worrying about were those pesky foreigners. Maybe it was, but it seemed to be going through a 'Leyland knows best' phase, so the increasing presence of the underfloor-engined Volvo B58, particularly among coach operators, should have been a wake-up call — but wasn't. A few B58s were bodied as buses, denying

sales to Leyland, and a B59 rear-engined bus was built for the UK, but failed to impress. Scania had given Leyland a bit of a fright around the time the Leyland National was launched by liaising with British bodybuilder Metro-Cammell to produce the Metro-Scania rear-engined citybus. It notched up a few significant protest sales but faded away when Scania and Metro-Cammell decided to concentrate on the double-deck market with the Metropolitan.

So what single-deckers were all the others buying? NBC, as we have seen, was Leyland National-land, all in poppy red or leaf green, and there were customers for the National among the Passenger Transport Executives and municipalities, as well as London Transport. But although all the PTEs bought Nationals, and London Transport became a significant customer, they were also taking advantage of the Government's generous New Bus Grant scheme and taking double-deckers in substantial numbers to eliminate non-standard types and spread one-person operation.

The PTEs did rock the Leyland boat though, possibly in protest, by buying Metro-Scanias (Merseyside, SELNEC) and Mercedes-Benz O.305s (SELNEC, albeit only two). And they also stuck to Leyland's more conventional fare, still available but intended mainly as coach chassis, West Yorkshire, in particular, buying Leopard and Tiger buses.

The mention of the Mercedes-Benz O.305s, a hugely successful type in its native Germany and elsewhere in Europe, underlines the fact that Continental manufacturers were eyeing the UK market.

Mercedes-Benz managed to get the two O.305s with Northern Counties bodies into the SELNEC fleet in 1973, but it would be nearly 20 years before it broke into the UK bus market with the O.405 and then the Citaro.

Also testing the UK bus market was Renault, which in 1988 offered its PR100 model in concert with Northern Counties. Just five were built for UK operators. Iveco also dabbled in the UK market with the TurboCity model, first as a rather ungainly double-decker and then with a single-deck version; again, few were built.

For some operators, low floor levels and wide entrances seemed to have little appeal. The Scottish Bus Group resisted the lure of the Leyland National for some years, preferring its well-tried Leyland Leopard/Alexander Y type combination — though from 1973 Leyland's grip on this market was challenged when SBG decided that a Gardner-engined Leopard would be a useful machine. Leyland wouldn't build one, so SBG went to Seddon, which was happy to develop the Pennine VII, an underfloor-engined model with the engineer's favourite power unit, the Gardner 6HLXB. For the next decade SBG dual-sourced between Leopards and Pennines for bus and coach work, though it did relent and buy some Nationals in 1977. However, the Leopard — and, later, the Tiger — continued to appeal to the more conservative municipal operators, some of whom remained deeply suspicious of the National.

One of the advantages of the National was its availability. As a mass-produced single-deck vehicle it was almost a matter of turning the Workington handle a little faster. So when Eastern Scottish needed buses urgently, 10 Nationals magically appeared. And although SBG engineers may have shared the industry's widespread concerns about the 510 engine, they realised that the National had a place as an urban bus, and over the next few years most SBG fleets would take Nationals — as well as Leopards and Pennines, of course. Even when the Leopard was no longer available, the group turned to Leyland's Tiger and helped to persuade Dennis to produce a Gardner-engined version of this, the Dorchester. Leyland eventually gave in and produced a Gardner-engined Tiger, and SBG did have the good grace to buy some.

By the mid-1980s the National had reached the end of the road, in spite of its relaunch as the National 2 in 1979 with the big 680 engine (and subsequently the 690, TL11H and Gardner units). Some 7,600 had been built, and although it received mixed reviews it showed that a spacious, easy-to-use single-decker was what many passengers wanted, even if the standard interior was a little sterile.

Below: **Stagecoach inherited Alexander P-type Leyland Tigers from Grimsby-Cleethorpes Transport. One is seen in Sheffield's Meadowhall bus station in 1995 alongside a Mainline Leyland-DAB artic.**

Above: The Scottish Bus Group continued to buy narrow-entrance, high-floor single-deckers until well into the 1980s. This is a rare Dennis Dorchester with 49-seat Alexander TE-type body, in East Kilbride in 1984.

Below: A late-model Leyland National 2, dating from 1985, working in Hove for Brighton & Hove.

Orders had dropped to a trickle by 1985, not necessarily because operators didn't want Nationals but because they weren't sure what — if anything — they should buy. Bus-service deregulation would take effect in October 1986, and, if the possibility of competition didn't offer enough uncertainties, the Government compounded things by commencing the sell-off of NBC. If bus operators were buying anything it was shoals of 'breadvan' minibuses to defend their territory and attack the enemy, real or imagined.

Leyland, of course, wasn't going to drop the National without having a replacement available. This, we learned, would be the Lynx, a bus that looked very different from the National, and was a very different animal. While the National was a fully integral bus, the Lynx was an underframe that could, in theory, support a range of bodies from a range of builders, even double-deckers. It also had the potential to be produced in shorter or longer versions, maybe even articulated. In practice, little of this happened.

The Lynx got off to a slow start, but a few substantial orders from operators like Caldaire and West Midlands Travel helped to get it going, and it achieved respectable sales of more than 1,000 between 1985 and 1992 — by which time the world had changed.

Below: Two Leyland Lynxes supplied in 1987 to Shearings for services in Greater Manchester, seen in Bolton bus station in 1988.

NBC was no more, so old loyalties had changed and new groupings were coming — and going — as the British bus industry reinvented itself. Even Leyland was no more, following its sale — first to its management in 1987 and then (with indecent haste, some suggested) to Volvo the following year. Volvo stated at the time that the Lynx was one of the Leyland models that interested it most, but that proved not to be the case, and the Lynx (and Volvo's B10R equivalent, never offered in the UK) were replaced by the Volvo B10B, which sold in respectable numbers.

By the time the Lynx went there were other rival models waiting in the wings. DAF, which had entered the UK market in the 1970s with coach chassis, burst onto the UK bus scene in 1988 with the SB220 — or rather Optare did, with the SB220-based Delta. Born in 1985 out of the ashes of Leyland's Roe body plant in Leeds, Optare was making a name for itself with stylish small buses, and the undeniably striking Delta body showed that single-deck buses didn't have to look like bricks. The model was usually known simply as the Optare Delta; DAF's contribution was somehow overlooked.

Scania had introduced its K- and N-series chassis in the 1980s, suitable for either single- or double-deck bodywork, and a later single-decker, introduced to the UK in 1994, was the L113, which became the basis for the low-floor Wright-bodied Axcess-ultralow.

Above: The Leyland Lynx could be found in small numbers in London. This is a 1989 London United example, at Richmond bus station.

Below: Despite proclaiming itself to be a low-floor bus this GM Buses North vehicle is actually a step-entrance Volvo B10B with Wright Endurance body. It is seen in Manchester when new in 1994.

Above: The DAF SB220/Optare Delta introduced stylish new looks for single-deck buses. This Delta is seen in Skipton in 1995 on ABC Travel's long route from Southport.

Below: Although at first glance this looks like later Scania/Wright low-floor buses this is a step-entrance N113CRB with Wright Endurance body, supplied to Midland Bluebird in 1994 and seen in Stirling.

Above: In 1993/4 Yorkshire Rider received a sizeable fleet of Scania N113CRBs and Volvo B10Bs, all with Alexander Strider bodywork. A Scania is pursued through Leeds by a Volvo in FirstBus days.

Below: Between 1995 and 1997 Oxford Bus Company bought 43 Volvo B10Bs with Plaxton Verde bodywork. This one is seen in 2003.

What had been Leyland's market was now anybody's. DAF's SB220, Volvo's B10B, Scania's L113, the Dennis Lance and the Mercedes-Benz O.405 all competed for big single-deck sales in the early 1990s, following Volvo's decision to retire the Lynx. Their rear-engined layouts and low frames made them comparatively easy to use in the days before true low-floor and low-entry buses became available.

Not that rear-engined lowish-floor models were to everybody's taste. Although the new and emerging groups were beginning to show their loyalties — Grampian liked Scanias, Badgerline Dennises — one group stuck to underfloor-engined chassis. Stagecoach's standard single-decker from 1992 was the Volvo B10M, fitted with Alexander PS-type body — to all intents and purposes an SBG Leopard/Y type reborn, though with a considerably lower floorline.

Never a slave to fashion, Stagecoach persevered with the B10M/PS until 1998, by which time the bus world had changed again. The Dennis Dart had introduced a new concept — a bus that could be anything from a big minibus to virtually a full-size bus. The other new concept was the stepless low-floor or low-entry bus, a type that had been around in Continental Europe for some years, but which became available to all with the Dart SLF. For a time it had seemed that high prices would ensure that low-floor buses would have only a limited appeal in Britain. The Dart changed all that, and there appeared a new breed of full-size single-deck low-floor chassis — the Dennis Dart SLF, Volvo B10L and B10BLE, Scania L113 and Neoplan N4014. So sales of the step-entrance single-decker, a genre that had served Britain since the late 1960s, petered out as operators introduced fleets of easy-access low-floor types, many of them developed from previous models.

No one type will probably ever corner the full-size single-deck market in the way that Leyland did with the National in the 1970s, or in the way Dennis cornered the midibus market in the 1990s and early 2000s, although Volvo's B7RLE is giving it a good try.

It is easy to write off models like the step-entrance B10B, L113 and SB220 (don't manufacturers give models names these days?) because the 'step change' to easy-access buses has apparently rendered them superfluous. Yet they continue to give good service in a range of fleets and represent one small step — well, often two shallow ones — on the way to low-floor buses.

Below: Grampian bought Mercedes-Benz O.405s between 1993 and 1997. The first batch had Wright Cityranger bodywork, as seen in 1995 in Union Street, Aberdeen.

Right: Stagecoach's Volvo B10M/Alexander PS buses can be found throughout the country. This 1996 example is seen in St Enoch Square, Glasgow, working for Stagecoach Glasgow.

Below: The step-entrance Dennis Dart heralded a major move towards midi-size step-entrance buses, particularly in London. This is a 1991 Dart with Carlyle Dartline body in the London United fleet, seen crossing Kingston Bridge.

Right: London was not a big market for full-size single-deckers in the 1990s, but in 1993 a batch of 13 Volvo B10Bs with Northern Counties Paladin bodywork was supplied to London Buses and branded for the 88 'Clapham Omnibus' route.

Barnsley in the 1950s

ROY MARSHALL first visited Barnsley in 1950. Here he takes a look back at the town's buses in the decade that followed.

Above: This fine Leyland Titanic TT5 was operated by Cawthorne of Barugh on a service between Barnsley and Woolley Colliery. It had a Roe body and had been new to Doncaster Corporation. The service was taken over by Yorkshire Traction in 1952.

Left: When Yorkshire Traction acquired Cawthorne's route it took over the Titanic along with this Foden PVD6 with Willowbrook body. It had started life as a Foden demonstrator.

Above: Camplejohn Bros of Darfield operated a service from there to Barnsley. In 1955 the company purchased this Atkinson demonstrator with Burlingham body, seen here in the following year. Camplejohn's services would be taken over by Yorkshire Traction in 1961.

Below: This is a 1959 view of a Weymann-bodied Guy Arab operated by Moseley of Barugh, on the service between Higham and Barnsley and advertising a local brew, Barnsley Bitter. The bus was new to Sheffield Transport. Moseley gave up bus operation in 1965 but continued running coaches.

Left: Larrett Pepper & Sons of Thurscoe was another operator to give up buses in the 1960s and concentrate on coaching. This rare bus is a Daimler Freeline with Burlingham body, dating from 1952. It was photographed in 1955.

Left: Rowe of Cudworth also ceased operating buses but continued running coaches, relinquishing its service between Cudworth and Barnsley in 1969. Operating on that service in 1955 was this unique vehicle, an ex-Yorkshire Woollen Leyland Tiger TS7 fitted with an AEC engine and a body, believed to date from the 1930s, that had been extensively rebuilt by Rowe before being mounted on this chassis in 1951.

Right: South Yorkshire Motors was one of the larger independents in Yorkshire and until 1950 had favoured Albions, represented by this Venturer CX37 in Barnsley on the company's service to Pontefract. It had a Strachans body, which had been the subject of a rebuild by the time of this 1959 photograph.

Top: County Motors, of Lepton, operated to Barnsley from Huddersfield, where this 1949 Roe-bodied Guy Arab III was photographed in 1952. The company was owned jointly by Yorkshire Traction and the independent West Riding business.

Above: Between 1943 and 1945 Yorkshire Traction purchased 25 utility Guy Arabs, all with Gardner 6LW engines. Photographed in 1956, this 1944 bus had a Northern Counties body.

Left: Typical of Yorkshire Traction's early postwar single-deckers was this 1947 Leyland Tiger PS1 with Weymann body. Another Tiger, but with Roe body, stands alongside.

Right: Deliveries to Yorkshire Traction in 1951 included 20 Leyland Royal Tigers. These were a mixture of 37-seat Windover-bodied coaches and, as seen here in 1956, 43-seat Brush-bodied buses.

Left: The service between Barnsley and Rotherham was operated jointly by Yorkshire Traction and Rotherham Corporation. Seen in 1951, this Corporation Bristol L6B with East Lancs body had been new the previous year.

Above: In 1955 Yorkshire Traction purchased a Beadle-Commer integral for evaluation alongside Leyland Tiger Cubs. It is seen on the Barnsley-Rotherham service in 1956, in which year it was joined by a second example. Both had shorter operating lives than the Leylands.

Below: Burrows of Wombwell operated a lengthy service between Leeds and Wath, a distance of 39 miles. The company's mixed fleet included this ex-London Transport AEC Regent, which had been fitted with a second-hand Strachans body. It is seen operating a Leeds duplicate in 1957.

The Metrobus in the West Midlands

The MCW Metrobus was built in the West Midlands, and more than 1,000 were supplied to the region's leading operator. **DAVID COLE** tells the story.

All photographs by David Cole

Birmingham in early 1978: a city still at the forefront of motor-vehicle manufacture and served by a Passenger Transport Executive keen to support local businesses when sourcing its vehicles. The Coventry-built Daimler Fleetline had long been the first choice of chassis, many with bodywork from the Washwood Heath plant of MCW, but this was changing. Not only had there been a need to multi-source to accelerate the replacement of vehicles unsuitable for one-man-operation, bringing in Bristol VRTs and Volvo Ailsas, but British Leyland had switched Fleetline production to its Lancashire factory in Leyland, ending the local connection. Delivery dates slipped badly in the mid-1970s, and it was late 1977 before the last of Birmingham's iconic postwar 'new look' buses, by then nearly 25 years old, could be replaced.

MCW had been early in the field of challenging Leyland's monopoly of chassis supply, working with Swedish manufacturer Scania to produce the Metro-Scania single-decker and, later, the Metropolitan double-decker. Each found its supporters, but many operators found them complex and thirsty. West Midlands PTE steered clear of the Anglo-Swedish model, taking just two — a single-decker for evaluation and then a refurbished double-deck prototype, which it had on loan during 1977. Then came the announcement that MCW would be offering a wholly Birmingham-built bus with the PTE's preferred Gardner engine and a Voith gearbox. Thus was born the MCW Metrobus.

In late March 1978 I received my first posting as a graduate engineer with British Gas, to a depot immediately across the railway complex from MCW's Washwood Heath works. One lunchtime soon afterwards I was passing the PTE's depot in Washwood Heath, and there it was — the first Metrobus, ready for a trial run. It was impressive, an impression strengthened by the revised WMPTE livery. The use of a greater area of blue (of a lighter shade than hitherto), with black window surrounds and skirt,

together with a lower cream band, marked a step change from the Birmingham-style livery that had been adopted by the PTE when it was created. At the time this had been further simplified to an uninspiring cream with blue lower panels, and it had not been helped by problems with the cream paint on some new Fleetlines which saw them take on a pink hue.

The body styling of the new MCW model adopted the clean-cut box approach; gone were the gentle curves and bustle of the Park Royal-inspired Fleetline body. As might have been expected, there was some family resemblance to the Metropolitan, including the use of an asymmetric windscreen, but without the heavy mouldings. There was also a likeness to the London Transport DMS body, many of which were built by MCW (and which would later make an unexpected appearance in the WMPTE fleet). Internally the Metrobus featured the autumnal colours of the era and accommodation for 73 seated passengers — a reduction of three compared with the Fleetlines then entering the WMPTE fleet.

Five pre-production vehicles, Nos 6831-5, were built for the WMPTE fleet for comparative trials planned with a similar number of Leyland's new B15 Titan. In the event it was to be several months before all of the latter (7001-5) were delivered, and initial comparisons were undertaken on Washwood Heath's route 94 between the first Metrobus, 6831, and Leyland Titan demonstrator FHG 592S. The second Metrobus, 6832, went to Coventry, where it entered service alongside WMPTE's last surviving half-cab buses, appropriately with MCW bodywork. Nos 6833 and 6834 went to the Black Country, to Dudley and Wolverhampton respectively, whilst 6835 would eventually double the Metrobus contingent at Washwood Heath. No 6833 appeared at the 1978 Sandwell rally, boldly proclaiming itself as 'the bus of the 1980s'.

In November 1978 a combined car and commercial-vehicle exhibition was held for the first time at the National Exhibition Centre, and 6835 appeared on the MCW stand alongside a Hong Kong example and a bare chassis. An extensive park-and-ride operation was put into place, including the use of an unopened section of the M42 motorway some two miles distant.

To operate this WMPTE provided a large fleet of recently delivered vehicles, including all four of the pre-production Metrobuses by then in service.

The Metrobus rapidly won orders, early production examples going to London Transport and to other PTEs, whilst WMPTE was still receiving its final Fleetlines and was planning to dual-source future orders with similar numbers of Titans and Metrobuses. Following the scaling-down of Titan production plans a smaller number of Volvo B55s was considered as an alternative, but the eventual outcome was significant numbers of Metrobuses and a small number of Leyland Nationals.

It was to be the autumn of 1979 before the first production vehicles from an initial order for 75 were delivered to WMPTE. The honour of placing the first batch into service went to Selly Oak depot, which had not operated any of the pre-production buses. It did, however, receive one of the Titans, giving it some experience of second-generation rear-engined vehicles. Selly Oak buses served the Bristol Road, one of the city's flagship routes and home to the dual-door 'Jumbo' Fleetlines. Less than 10 years old, the Park Royal bodies on these vehicles were giving serious cause for concern, and some had already been replaced by older Fleetlines from Coventry. Fifteen Metrobuses, starting a new number series at 2001, entered service from November 1979, supported in the role of 'Jumbo' replacement by a fleet of ex-London DMSs — with MCW bodies, of course.

The production Metrobuses were immediately distinguishable from the pre-production batch by a livery change. Out went the black window surrounds, whilst the position of the lower cream band and the format of the fleetname were also changed. To test

alternative power units, two additional vehicles equipped with Rolls-Royce engines were delivered around the same time, taking the numbers 7006/7, which followed on from the Leyland Titans in WMPTE's original number series.

The second batch of production vehicles went to Coventry, where old Atlanteans, including ex-Hull examples, had enabled the remaining half-cabs to be removed a few months earlier. Deliveries then continued apace, examples being allocated across the PTE area, including to the remaining ex-Midland Red depots. Within three years a fleet of 435 production Metrobuses (2001-2435) had been amassed, all but a few to the PTE's standard specification. The exceptions included 20 vehicles equipped with Rolls-Royce engines (2226-45) and allocated to Birmingham's Acocks Green depot, plus 2102, which featured an early example of an electronic destination screen.

Elsewhere, significant numbers of Metrobuses continued to be delivered to London, while export success had been achieved with a modified three-axle version for Hong Kong. This redesign work paved the way for the Mk II Metrobus, a simplified design with significantly fewer individual components compared with the original, which became referred to as the Mk I. Externally the trademark asymmetric windscreen was replaced by a symmetrical one derived from the Hong Kong design, whilst the doors were changed, a narrower rear door leaf giving more gangway clearance when open.

Left: WMPTE's first production Metrobuses entered service on Birmingham's Bristol Road route late in the autumn of 1979. With poor weather and construction work taking place at the outer end of the route it was unusual to find them as clean as 2013, passing through Selly Oak in February 1980.

Right: One of the few non-standard Mk I Metrobuses in the WMPTE fleet was 2102, fitted with a dot-matrix destination display. By October 1985, when this photograph was taken in Birmingham's Corporation Street, it had received a repaint, losing its black skirt.

Left: Metrobuses for other operators were often to be seen on test around Birmingham. One of the most impressive was China Motor Bus ML1, the first 'Jumbo' Metrobus, seen at Stonebridge Island (between Birmingham and Coventry) in March 1981.

Standard Mk I Metrobus 2389, repainted without a black skirt, in Navigation Street, Birmingham, in August 1984.

The first WMPTE Mk II, 2436, received significant local publicity when new, including an appearance at the 1982 Sandwell Historic Vehicle Parade. Delivery of Mk IIs proceeded apace and by the time of the 1982 Motor Show had reached 2543, which featured on the MCW stand. During 1985 the total of Mk IIs surpassed that of the Mk Is, and a fleet of 475 standard examples (2436-2910) were in stock by the end of the year, following which, with deregulation looming, there was a lull in deliveries.

On the Mk IIs the standard livery was simplified with the dropping of the black skirt, although a varied fleet image was presented by a growing number of all-over advertising liveries. Several vehicles received a special Bus & Coach Council campaign livery expressing concern at the deregulation proposals — probably a pointless exercise, given the then Government's attitude to the bus and to public ownership in general. The PTE's own campaign against deregulation continued right up until the legislation was passed by Parliament, and in a final protest the campaign-liveried Metrobuses took part in a colourful parade around Birmingham city centre before being exhibited in an open day at Perry Barr depot.

In the late 1970s and early 1980s most PTEs were looking at rail-based schemes to improve transport in their areas, and WMPTE was no exception, introducing the cross-city rail link and promoting plans for a light-rail network which was to be nearly two decades in gestation. Looking for further opportunities, the PTE had its attention caught by developments in Germany. The city of Essen had introduced a guided-bus system,

providing most of the benefits of light rail in a form which was flexible through the use of almost-standard rubber-tyred vehicles and which minimised the road space required for segregated sections of route.

Birmingham's route 65 was subsequently chosen for the UK's first guided busway, which was also to be the world's first to feature double-deckers. Severe local opposition was experienced to the building of the guided section of the route, as this involved the loss of many mature trees which had been established on the central reservation following the end of tramway operation some 30 years earlier. The guided section was on the quiet suburban section of the route where it could be considered only as a demonstration; on the more congested sections towards the city centre improvements were limited to conventional bus lanes and improved bus-stop facilities.

Not surprisingly the Metrobus was chosen as the vehicle for Tracline 65, as the project became known. Fourteen Mk IIs were built with additional chassis strengthening to cope with the stresses expected from the guidewheels installed immediately behind the front wheels. Numbered in a new series as 8101-14, they were distinguished externally by a bold silver and black livery and equipped with dot-matrix destination displays. There were two versions of the latter — provision for a service number and single line destination within a standard aperture, or an enlarged aperture with space for two lines of destination to be displayed. Two key features of the Tracline vehicles had earlier been trialled on standard Mk II Metrobuses, 2686 being the first vehicle with guide wheels and 2791 fitted with a dot-matrix destination display.

Launched in August 1984, the system appeared to work well, although the route had limited potential for passenger growth, and within two years consideration

was being given to its future after deregulation. Sunday services were not considered viable by the PTE's new arm's-length operating company, and these were not registered, probably with mistaken confidence that they would be regained upon tendering, as no other operator could provide appropriate vehicles. In the event the PTE's tender specification did not rule out normal vehicle operation on the parallel roadway, and the tendered journeys passed to Midland Red West. Passengers now faced the confusion of stops on the road or on the busway, depending upon the time of day, and the writing was on the wall for the guided operation. The last journeys ran early in 1987, following which the special Metrobuses were repainted into standard livery, renumbered 2961-74 and dispersed around the network.

A more positive approach to deregulation by the PTE's operating company was demonstrated by the development of a network of limited-stop interurban routes across the West Midlands and out into Staffordshire. At a time when the industry was focusing strongly on minibuses the order for 50 dual-purpose Mk II Metrobuses for this operation (2911-2960) was significant to MCW, which had lost out in the 1986 London orders. Featuring 66 coach seats and carpets, these Timesaver Metrobuses stood out in their mainly

silver livery with bold branding which was facilitated, on the front panel, by a lower-mounted destination screen.

Delivery spanned the formation of the new arm's-length company, West Midlands Travel, whose large logo was to replace the small WM branding. Initially the WMPTE blue livery was retained, but the silver of the Timesavers had made an impression, and a silver-based livery was soon introduced across the fleet. This evolved over several years. The silver was replaced by better-wearing grey shades which gradually became lighter, the roof and upper-deck window surrounds once again became blue, and a red band edged in white provided additional relief below the lower saloon windows. With minor changes to the edging bands this livery proved to be the longest-lived of any carried by Metrobuses in the West Midlands.

West Midlands Travel soon announced its first order for double-deckers, 150 Metrobuses, which was welcomed in securing local employment. Sometimes described as Mk IIa vehicles, these vehicles (2975-3124) had a number of external differences in addition to the new silver livery. The nearside service-number display was replaced by a longer number-and-destination display box (often reduced in later life), and the rear upper-deck emergency exit was fully glazed. The first examples entered service in 1988 on Birmingham's route 50, destined to be the city's premier route for investment during the next decade.

All, however, was not well. By the time the Metrobus fleet had reached the 1,000 mark earlier examples were apparently giving cause for concern, and several,

Right: The 963 along the Bristol Road to Gannow was one of the beneficiaries of the coach-seated Timesaver Metrobuses. No 2935 is seen in Longbridge in November 1986.

Left: Several shades of grey and silver were applied in the transition period from WMPTE blue and cream to Travel West Midlands' blue, light grey and red. In grey livery, Coventry-based Mk II 2615 is seen close to the city's railway station in February 1990.

Right: Following the trials with 2102, 2791 was selected as another testbed for dot-matrix destination displays. Carrying the later standard livery and working from Walsall depot, it is seen climbing to Birmingham's Bull Ring in May 1993.

Top: Once silver and grey became the standard fleet livery a new blue livery with gold lettering was chosen to differentiate the Timesaver fleet. One of the Metrobuses to receive the scheme was 2933, seen climbing Birmingham's Bull Ring in June 1993. This road has since disappeared beneath Birmingham's Selfridges store.

Above: No 2993 was the 1,000th Metrobus delivered to WMPTE and its successors, although earlier vehicles were being withdrawn when it arrived. In recognition of the milestone it carried the fleet number 1000 for a short period, including whilst exhibited at the 1988 NEC show. One of many Mk IIa Metrobuses to be allocated to Wolverhampton, it is seen in its home city — then still a town — in March 1989.

including most of the pre-production batch, were sold before all of the so-called Mk IIa batch entered service. Early sales found homes with new owners including Ensignbus, Yorkshire Traction and Stevensons of Uttoxeter.

There were also problems at MCW. The Metrorider minibus had proved successful, but the company's strength was always in building large batches of standardised vehicles, and these large orders had all but disappeared. Route tendering had meant the end of annual London orders, and the only Metrobuses for the capital after 1985 were small batches for Ensignbus and London Buses' autonomous Harrow Buses unit. With strong railway orders putting pressure on capacity at Washwood Heath it was not too surprising when the end of MCW bus production was announced.

The final vehicles of West Midlands Travel's Mk IIa batch were caught up in the cessation of production, and delivery extended into 1990 amidst legal wrangling over warranty and quality issues. One vehicle of the batch, 3107, was never taken into stock, eventually passing, with the design rights, to Optare, whence evolved the Spectra. From Optare 3107 was sold on to Capital Citybus, finishing its UK career with First in Manchester, but in a final twist to its life story it was to join some original WMPTE vehicles in being exported to Sri Lanka in 2005 as part of the Asia Bus Response campaign following the tsunami on Boxing Day 2004.

With the final entry into service of the Mk IIa batch a total of 1,130 Metrobuses had entered service with WMPTE or its successor. Although West Midlands Travel's purchasing policy for new vehicles now switched mainly to single-deckers, the long-term future for much of the Metrobus fleet was assured when a refurbishment programme was instituted. Much of the work was below the surface, replacing and strengthening the underframe, whilst externally the most obvious change was a reduction in size of the lower-deck rear window on Mk II vehicles and a relocation of the rear registration number plate, providing space for additional advertising. Most of the work was undertaken by Marshall of Cambridge, whose advertising claimed that nine Metrobuses could be refurbished for a further 10 years' life for the price of two new vehicles. Originally planned to encompass 1,100 vehicles, the refurbishment programme was abandoned before all of the fleet had been dealt with, and as a result early disposals appeared random across the Mk I and Mk II fleets.

In 1991 West Midlands Travel was the subject of a management and employee buy-out, an event well publicised to customers with 13 Metrobuses finished in a dark-green livery adorned with gold 'employee-owned' lettering. Following the merger with National Express in 1995, a new era commenced in 1996

Mk I	
6831-6834	SDA 831-834S
6835	WDA 835T
7006,7007	BOM 6, 7V
2001-2090	BOK 1-90V
2091-2275	GOG 91-275W
2276-2325	KJW 276-325W
2326-2435	LOA 326-435X

Mk II	
2436-2475	NOA 436-475X
2476-2610	POG 476-610Y
2611-2667	ROX 611-667Y
2668-2735	A668-735 UOE
2736-2772	A736-772 WVP
2773-2795	B773-795 AOC
2796-2860	B796-860 AOP
2861-2886	B861-886 DOM
2887-2910	C887-910 FON
2911-2960	D911-960 NDA

Mk II Tracline 65 (batch later renumbered 2961-2974)

8101-8114	A101-114 WVP

Mk IIa	
2975-2989	E975-989 VUK
2990-2999	F990-999 XOE
3000-3021	F300-321 XOF
3022-3103	F22-103 XOF
3104-3124*	G104-124 FJW

* 3107 not taken into stock

Above: Following the management and employee buy-out in late 1991 13 Metrobuses received this green and gold scheme, complete with home-depot branding. Hartshill's 3042 is seen in Dudley in May 1993.

In 1996/7 the heritage-liveried Metrobuses were often to be found at rallies and special events. Birmingham, Wolverhampton, West Bromwich and Coventry examples are seen on display at the Aston Manor Road Transport Museum in July 1996.

when the operation was rebranded Travel West Midlands, the remaining Metrobuses gaining the new, smaller TWM fleetnames. Also in 1996 Metrobuses were again chosen as the basis for celebration, this time of the company's heritage, examples appearing in traditional Birmingham, Coventry, Walsall, West Bromwich and Wolverhampton municipal liveries, launched at a snow-covered Black Country Museum. Several of these liveries would be long-lived, the Wolverhampton example, in particular, subsequently receiving a further repaint into an older livery style.

The new standard Travel West Midlands livery of white with red and blue diagonal bands was not applied to Metrobuses in the main fleet, but the style was adopted for an example transferred to the Travel Merry Hill operation, with green and blue diagonals. The dual-purpose vehicles in the Private Charter fleet, several of which had lost their destination equipment, also gained the new livery, as did 2939, converted as an open-topper. This was the second open-top conversion to serve its original owner, Mk I 2028 having been so treated in the early 1990s. However, several of the Metrobuses which had been sold off early became long-lived open-toppers with City Sightseeing. A number of the dual-purpose vehicles were later converted to driver-training buses in a white livery, most migrating to the Travel London operation.

The arrival of low-floor double-deckers in quantity meant the run-down of the Metrobus fleet, and the Mk I was eliminated in 2003. By late 2005 the Metrobus had been displaced from most major corridors into Birmingham, but significant numbers, mainly over-20-year-old refurbished vehicles but also some Mk IIa and dual-purpose vehicles, were still required in the Black Country towns and for peak-hour duties.

Despite the reduction in numbers the Metrobus was still capable of breaking new ground in the 21st century. In 2002 TWM's operations in Coventry were relaunched as Travel Coventry, its vehicles, including a number of Metrobuses, gaining sky-blue relief in lieu of red. In Solihull a new service from the station to a business park on a greenfield site alongside the M42 was started with branded Metrobuses, and in Birmingham the 26 Saver Bus route was extended and upgraded to double-deck operation with branded Mk IIa Metrobuses featuring yellow relief.

That the refurbishment programme had been a worthwhile exercise was surely demonstrated by the popularity of 20-plus-year-old vehicles on the second-hand market, a number of operators amassing significant fleets. In the case of Travel de Courcey in Coventry some of them, smartly repainted and route-branded, were to compete with their original owner on a new city service launched in 2005. Surprisingly, more than 25 years after the model's appearance, this was one of the most significant uses of Metrobuses by

Below: **In the late 1990s a number of the Metrobuses with coach-type seating were transferred to Travel West Midlands' Private Charter fleet. With fixed destination display, 2927 awaits the return of its party in the heart of the Lickey Hills in September 2002.**

another operator in the West Midlands. Previously, Stevensons' examples, particularly its former MCW Dublin demonstrator, F181 YDA, had appeared on its Birmingham services, and Coastal Liner had run ex-London examples between Dudley and Wolverhampton.

Travel West Midlands appears likely to retain Metrobuses on specific duties for some time, several examples having received repaints in the middle of this decade. Otherwise the future of the Metrobus in the West Midlands will be in preservation. Already a number of Mk Is, including a pre-production vehicle and a Rolls-Royce-engined example, have been restored, whilst Aston Manor Road Transport Museum has acquired one of the Tracline vehicles, 8110, which is being restored as far as possible to its condition as delivered. It will gain guidewheels for display, but test-running on the more recent guided busways will not be possible, the necessary underframe strengthening having been removed at refurbishment.

Above: Travel Coventry was launched in 2002, the red in the Travel West Midlands livery being changed to sky blue, the colour of the local football team. New low-floor double-deckers and Citaro artics replaced some of the city's Metrobuses, but 2840, seen in the city centre, was one of a significant number still serving in May 2005.

Left: Saver Bus route 26 was launched with Leyland Lynxes but in 2006 was extended and upgraded to double-deck operation with yellow-banded Metrobuses. One of the vehicles involved, 3028, is seen in Birmingham's Old Square in June 2006, by which time some of the yellow had succumbed to the bus wash.

Above: Stevensons' Metrobuses were for several years a familiar sight in Birmingham. Alongside examples from several PTEs Stevensons also operated F181 YDA, the demonstrator provided to Dublin in 1988. This vehicle was a regular performer on the 112 Birmingham-Burton service but is seen in May 1989 on the shuttle service for Lichfield Bower.

Below: In the autumn of 2005 Coventry-based Travel de Courcey launched a new cross-city service competing with Travel Coventry. The vehicles chosen were former Travel West Midlands Metrobuses including one-time Tracline vehicle 2961, seen in October 2006 outside the Coventry Transport Museum, smartly repainted and branded for the service.

Of damsels and digressions

ROBERT E. JOWITT — continuing from an extravaganza recently appearing in *Classic Bus Yearbook* — renders an analytic criticism of his essays in *Buses Annual* and *Buses Yearbook* over 35 eventful years.

All photographs by the author unless otherwise credited

Not infrequently, when writing for the pages of *Buses Yearbook*, I have indulged in the habit of digression, or straying from the path of my subject. I intend to do so again, in starting these present passages, although, as the reader will see, the digression is not entirely remote from the purpose of the narrative.

Now in the works of that great English novelist Enid Blyton, when she has several books forming a series, she tells us that each book may be read by itself though the characters will be found again and again. She solves the problems this might present to the uninformed reader by means of quick character sketches in each volume following the first; thus, in a tale of jolly school-girls, *'The girl* [probably pronounced 'gel'] *was a genius at maths and music and a complete duffer at everything else'* [such as *what*, the reader wonders] or, in a daring tale of adventure where children rush willy-nilly without a second thought into perilous places such as derelict mines — a very bad example to today's children when such folly is plainly politically incorrect and probably forbidden by EU directives — we find our hero thus: *'The boy was wonderful at attracting animals, he usually had a squirrel in his pocket or a mouse in his shirt-collar* [what a laundry bill!] *…'*, which reminds me of a real-life example …

W. G. Wills, author of one of the most famous and popular Victorian drawing-room ballads, 'I'll sing thee Songs of Araby', is recorded as having retired at an early age almost perpetually to bed, in squalor, surrounded by stray cats, monkeys and other 'unclean animals'. I may say that sometimes, hailing an unsmiling morn, I have had occasion to envy him and even once or twice to emulate him, though my cats come respectably from the RSPCA and I have not risen — or sunk — to monkeys.

If I make remark on this worthy artist it is however only to press the point that far from idling abed under cat I am up with pen in hand writing a digression for *Buses Yearbook*, and the reason for the reference to the works of dear Enid is that this article upon which I am now engaged is written to some extent as the second part of an article which has recently appeared in *Classic Bus Yearbook*, which is to say that both articles are on the same subject, involving the same heroes and heroines and buses, but each article can be read quite separately.

I do not propose to provide herewith much clue of what I have written in *CBY* — you can go out and buy it, can't you, or at the very worst borrow it — save only to say that therein, and herein, I am celebrating the anniversary of having been writing for *Buses Annual*, then *Buses Yearbook*, and, later, *Classic Bus Yearbook*, for 35 years.

This anniversary seems to me to provide a suitable juncture in which to go back through the pages and to read again what I wrote in bygone years (and more recently too), to study what has changed in the scenes I recorded then, and to criticise myself and my style over words for which perhaps I now might blush, and to append (if I am allowed) a few words which at the time were trimmed by editorial whim (though it is no use my putting up all of them, for some would certainly be trimmed again!) and a further few words which I myself left undone when I ought to have done them.

Obviously over three-and-a-half decades and many subjects and themes there is no simple rationale by which the topics may be ordered, so I shall simply start at the beginning and see whither doth the wind blow us.

Before I proceed further, however, I give notice of abbreviations I propose, such as *BA* for *Buses Annual* and *BY* for *Buses Yearbook* followed by the year applying to the volume in question, while where mention of *Classic Bus Yearbook* may be made this will obviously be *CBY*, but followed by its 'fleet number', as it does not (save for the original 1995 edition) admit to a specific year.

My first offering, then, was for *BA 1972*, the subject being *l'autobus*, which is French for 'the bus', a subject upon which, despite a general apathy for (or even antipathy towards) buses, I was completely enamoured.

Left: **Last days of la belle époque in Paris, 1970, with 1935 Renault TN4F 3267 still in active service (and soon to be in Jowitt preservation), captured at full-speed — all of 20mph — on the upgrade of the Rue de Rome from the back platform of the preceding 1936 TN4H. Arguably, in Jowitt's view, the finest bus photo he ever took.**

L'autobus was as addictive to me as those fat yellow Boyards maize-papered cigarettes, now long since outlawed by the EU as too deadly. I well remember lighting one on the rear platform of a 1936 Renault TN4H at the terminus of the Paris route 80 at the Mairie du XVème and smoking it right through to the far terminus of the Mairie du XVIIIème. Due to some peculiarity of the paper the cigarette, though going well, left the paper largely, though with burn-holes, intact, and to this day it is stuck in my diary. As for the buses, I elected to describe them as, according to current French practice — *ancien, moderne* and *standard*. The *anciens* consisted principally, in Paris, of the recently retired 1935/6 Renaults, the *modernes* were partly the postwar generation which were soon to follow the TNs into oblivion and partly the Chaussons which in other cities and rural areas still seemed widespread —

though I suspect with hindsight that they too were close to death — while of the *standards* I had little to say, reckoning them too hideous to merit comment.

In all these three categories, however, I was to return later in these pages.

The Paris Renault TNs, the 1935 TN4F with bodywork already 19 years behind the times when it took to the streets and the aerodynamic follower with the same engine, the 1936 TN4H, were among the most incredible buses you could ever wish to see, both by virtue of design and longevity. Over the years they have slipped not infrequently into these pages, but principally in regard to my own efforts at preserving them, 'Parisiennes in Exile', *BA 1977*.

At that date, though I was already in possession of three buses, I had never managed all three on the road at once, and I promised my readers that when this was

Left: Last days of the 1935 Renault TN4F in Paris, early 1970. The route number is slipping from its holds, probably rusted away. Conductor Leopold, left, shudders in the non-uniform coat (and a scarf) which exposure on open-platforms demanded in winter, while he and driver Hammes are both smoking during a break at Place Pigalle ... as, no doubt, was Jowitt. Those were the days!

Below: Robert E. Jowitt at the apogee of his Paris-bus-preservation career, 1980, with three active Renaults behind him (not a scene, alas, long to last!) — 1933 TN6A 2679, 1935 TN4F 3267, 1936 TN4H 3380. Tim Nicholson / Robert E. Jowitt collection

achieved I would hold a party. In truth it was achieved, in 1980, and 20 years to the day from when I had first taken a photo of a Paris bus, 3267, the bus which proved to be the first I collected!

I, with a crew of faithful followers, took all three to the Grand Transport Extravaganza at Crich Tramway Museum in 1980 and 1981 — where we had already been operating a rival Extravaganza service to the trams with one or two buses for several years — which proved to be the apotheosis of efforts by my Compagnie des Anciens Autobus en Angleterre, for from then on it became increasingly difficult to operate at all, with, little by little, soaring fuel and insurance costs, spiralling bureaucratic and MoT hassle, and decay and ageing of vehicles and Chief Mechanical Engineer and owner. To which was added the rash purchase of an extra TN4H, English-preserved and totally rotten.

A move from Hampshire, their early expatriate home, was to Herefordshire, where the buses lived in a lovely barn, and then on to the Isle of Wight, where they might have had a new shed built for them … but the inherited shares which would have built it were made over to me on a certain 11 September … and blown apart! I count myself as lucky now if I can have one bus to follow Vectis routes … and for how much longer?

As for the *moderne* and *standard* … On the Chausson I dwelt fondly, even adoringly, retrospectively and possibly with some slight inaccuracy — for the identification of the various types is a matter apparently mind-boggling even to the most serious French enthusiast — in 'Pig-Snout and her Younger Sisters' in *BY 1991*. Meanwhile, after an almost maudlin essay on French trolleybuses, 'A Meditative Meal' (*BA 1984*), I was dwelling on my conversion to the charms of the *standard*, despite its dreadful curved windscreen and the slaughter it wrought in the streets of Paris. In *BA 1986* I told how I learned to love the beast, in *BY 1991* I was perforce lamenting its impending decline.

It may be worth noting here that originally the *standard* came in two forms, offered by Berliet and Saviem; the former, despite attempts at double-deckers and midi-buses, fell fast by the wayside compared with the integral construction of the Saviem SC10 which lasted, even if later re-styled with even more offensive front end, long enough almost to achieve Leyland National life.

Below: One of the celebrated breed of so-called 'pig-snout' Chaussons c1950, heading with difficulty towards Lyon through the streets of St Genix sur Giers, Savoie, in July 1960.

Above: Chaussons in all their cross-country glory. Autocars Granger of Saint Étienne, Loire, about to set out for Rive de Gier in 1960.

Left: The rural Chausson was adapted, not necessarily quite suitably for the purpose, as an urban bus; here an example in Metz with extra central entrance ... but not much headroom for standees.

While still on the Continent of Europe I think I must state that my accounts of travels therein have always proved to me among the more satisfactory of my entries ... and particularly those which studied the charms of Lisbon and Porto. The archaic tram systems, with an attendant chorus, in Lisbon, of mirror-image AEC double-deckers, and, in Porto, of Edwardian narrow-gauge steam railways and double-deck trolleybuses, along with many wines and bewitching maidens, winning if never won, brought me to what I deem my most lyrical vein. I could add that, having lately been reading the works of Damon Runyan (of 'Guys & Dolls' fame), I wrote the first of these essays entirely in the present tense, including, for example, 'Lisbon is largely destroyed in 1755 by an earthquake ...' which was edited into the past tense. See *BA 1980* and *BA 1987* and the first 'CBY'. Tram systems survive today in both cities, but either drastically modernised or with the ancient cars running as 'heritage' services. I think I am unlikely to revisit.

Thus now, even if Continental influence or derelict Paris buses may slip in here and there, let me turn my

Above: A classic Standard of the early days, the short-lived Berliet PBR, here in Bordeaux in 1972.

Right: Mirror-image in Lisbon, 1976, with the cab of an AEC Regent III.

attention to my more patriotic essays.

Of King Alfred in my own (and the monarch's) native city of Winchester (though I was actually born in his birthplace, Wantage, then in Berkshire) I wrote of recent regal demise in *BA 1975*, and King Alfred buses have inserted themselves on occasion ever since. Likewise Winchester's other principal operator, Hants & Dorset, received attention at various dates, mainly in '47 Varieties' (*CBY 7*). So also did Mary, whom I travelled with or saw off on both operators in the late 1950s in unrequited love. I have never seen her since, and I guess she is not a reader of bus books, otherwise she might have contacted me to say how touched she is that I still remember her.

Girls, I have to admit, have featured much in my works. Unknown girls, due to my particular art form of photographing buses and girls in the streets, occur constantly in pictures — notably in *BA 1974* under the title 'Buses and Birds' and again in *BA 1985* in 'Skirt', neither of which terms I would estimate as 'socially correct' today, but a number of 'real' girls emerge in my writings, due to the bus journeys we shared.

Among the most attractive of these was another who evidently never read bus books, starring in what I counted at the time and still count now as perhaps my best masterpiece in all the series, 'Birmingham Sessions, Impressions and Digressions' (*BA 1983*). Note that the word 'digressions' was in the title, the first time, I dare say, that I admitted to the vice. One of the digressions was about my beloved dog Peter, already known in earlier articles; but the principal digression featured a visit in my 1936 Renault to Leicester to publicise the opening of a new hotel, wherein I met a telephone-switchboard girl. At the time I said only that her name rhymed with Irene, as in the famous old American song 'Irene Goodnight'. I have been asked since several times — or at least once — what was in truth her name, and this long afterwards I might admit that it was Noreen, or Noreen Bensley, of Wigston Fields, near Leicester, whither I drove her when the day's publicity was done, in the Renault.

She was a classic Pre-Raphaelite beauty. I was convinced I was seriously in love with her, but I had to take my bus back to the (then) Metro-Scania-filled Leicester depot where it was privileged to dwell during the tour, with only a vague promise from her that she and I might meet again in Paris, from whence, I must suppose because of the bus, she believed I hailed.

Far left: **Typical King Alfred study.** Stockbridge outstation driver Harold Davis (known as 'rat-catcher', for his out-of-hours pursuits) with habitual roll-up to his lips, in the last days of King Alfred c1972, with 1962 Leyland Leopard/Willowbrook 413 — among the first of the 36ft-long buses — in Winchester Broadway on the Stockbridge 'eight-ninths' service.

Left: **Unknown charmer in Winchester,** with typically elephanted rear of a Hampshire Bus Bristol LH6L/ECW, in the mid-1980s. Winchester was said at that time to be the most affluent city in England.

Right: **Three generations in Birmingham,** as described with enthusiasm by Jowitt in Buses Annual 1983. The mother with the push-chair may well now be a grandmother.

We never met again, either in Paris or Leicester. But, 'Noreen Goodnight', I cherish your memory still!

Of other bus-joys in Leicester, having promised then, in 1983, that I would write of them again in *BA 1999* if it should appear, verily I did (though by then it was a 'BY'), if only in the usual digression … in this case from the topic of Bath … which city itself appears again later herein!

As for Birmingham, outside the digressions, most of it is architecturally unrecognisable now, and the buses of the West Midlands long gone.

Far more serious than Noreen, however, and a decade or more before, was Carol of Bournemouth, my first really intimate girl-friend. Lest I be accused of wallowing too much in sentimental attachments let me state that our respected editor Brown himself dwelt in a bus-orientated article — though I no longer recall in which 'BA' it appeared — on some maiden behind the walls of a nurses' hostel. (Will he cut out that sentence?) Apart from my original falling-in-love, the details first appearing in *BA 1981* in 'Blissful Dreams of Long Ago' and enlarged upon in the latest 'CBY' (even if I said I wasn't going to tell anything here of what I wrote there), Carol has turned up again and again, from 'Blissful Dreams' and elsewhere — via 'The Primrose Path' (*CBY 2*) to my epic on Southampton

'The Yellow Dog and the Floating Bridge' (*BY 2001*) and as the principal heroine in the melodramatic 'The Last Thing on My Mind' in *CBY 9*. Needless to say, the Southampton then described is vanished without trace, but I delight to note that, though Carol and I were torn apart by Papal whim — and another woman — in 1964 (and to my eternal regret), she and I still, if not very often, write to each other.

A more recent charmer, a lady from far foreign parts, described as M — a title on which I do not propose further to elucidate — had star billing in 'The Last Sunday Bus to Potter Heigham' (*BY 2006*). She returned, alas, to the shores whence she came, probably never to return, leaving me bereft. It so happens that this article, apart from M, suffered a — to my mind — drastic editorial cull by Mr Brown. It has ever been my habit, while writing of my travels, to describe the people I meet and the conversations in which we indulge.

Long before I read the works of Paul Theroux, who is the past master in this genre, I was heading day-to-day passages in my diary of 1963 explorations of German trams and light railways with, apart from geographical notations, such titles as 'The Mad Priest' and 'The Immoral Aristocrat' and recording conversations with such notables. Neither space nor relevance will allow of further explanation of these persons, but I must beg our editor to include the following chopped-out passage from 'Potter Heigham'.

May I say that I believe that there is no point at all in writing about bus travel if it is to recount only boring details about boring buses, and thus I feel entitled to enlarge on the delights encountered at the end of the journey …

The butcher's shop at Horning, apart from an elderly gent in the background, was in charge of a young lady who, if not of Pre-Raphaelite beauty, was a most comely and amiable person. With the misfortune of never ascertaining her name I shall hereafter describe her as H, while adding that the butcher's shop displayed not only sundry hideous meats but also choice loaves and veg.

So, "Sandwiches," says H, when our eyes have fastened on a choice loaf, "yes, I can do you some sandwiches … with anything you like …"

"Anything?" said I, sensing a kindred spirit.

"No, not with teabags!"

We settle on ham and red pepper, and H retires to sundry cutting machines to achieve the desired results.

Then, REJ, "We'd better have one of those kitchen rolls too …"

H, resourcefully, "If it's only for the sandwiches …" and tears a handsome strip off the roll intended for butchering operations.

"But not with teabags!" say I.

"No!"

Later, H, as we pass again by the butcher's, is busily engaged in conversation with a van-delivery man. Regardless, I state: "Not with teabags."

"No, not with teabags!"

Later again, on our return, with sandwiches partly consumed, H is lolling, dare I say voluptuously, outside on the butcher's window sill, smoking a cigarette.

"I shall never forget," say I, "the teabag sandwiches …"

"Not with teabags," says H firmly and, after some reflection … for which I shall never know why … "and not with lemon curd either!!!" and then M and I with return-tickets catch a First-box back to Norwich …

M and I ate the last remains of H's sandwiches changing trains next morning at Ely …

In the final paragraphs of this tale — almost as lyrical, I think, as my earlier Portuguese efforts, last moment of M seen off on a South West Train — I made mention, not editorially excluded, of the articulated buses in Southampton, though they themselves, I found, were already excluded from the scene. M herself, in my company at a King Alfred running day, had eagerly purchased a copy of *BA 2004* with my words on 'Round the Bend' or the delights of articulated buses.

At the time of indulging in this essay I expressed the hope, if vaguely, that I might achieve encountering ex-Paris, subsequently Bordeaux, three-section mega-buses. This, like many another armchair-travel dream, failed to materialise, and probably is now nothing but a dream; but, apparently, a dream which might come to life, these days, elsewhere.

Meanwhile, in pursuit of this theme, to cap my stories on the realms of model buses (*CBY 12*) I have purchased, at sale price of £2.50 each, three Chinese three-axle *double-deck* articulateds. Of these I propose to keep one intact and to cut up the others to make one normal bus and one three-section double-deck artic. Likewise I shall remain, hereinafter, awaiting confirmation if either of these thoroughly unlikely forms have ever been seen on the roads … even in China!

I will return to the charge of the now-acceptable form of articulated bus on British streets in a subsequent paragraph, but, before this, though it is plainly not possible to cover all the articles of 35 years' effort, I wish to return to a couple in a rather different vein. These were 'Bus driving 'ell' in *BY 1997* and 'Schools' the following year, dwelling upon my learning to drive buses 'for real' rather than merely ancient Paris specimens.

Again this is a topic which has slipped in elsewhere in my writings, but I still wish to repeat that, even while driving buses through some of the most beautiful scenery in England, or, to be precise, the Welsh borders of Herefordshire, every day looking different under varying skies, it was an utter torment to suffer horrible little brats whose mothers would one day complain about the parlous condition of the buses — not, perhaps, entirely unjustified in certain cases, heavens, boiling over on a steep up-grade and with no brakes on a fiercer descent! — and then the next day complain that I was too drastic in bidding the little horrors to desist from creating appalling distractions, plastic bottles falling on my head, far more dangerous than any vehicle defects.

The day I told the beasts I was quitting (they are probably now respectable citizens or else in jail — could I dare to suppose or hope the latter?) the nasty little Bryn and the horrid little Kat danced together with joy in the road when they left the bus; I would have danced with them, had it not been beneath my dignity and that I must not leave the driving seat …

Moving on, and touring on what had now, abandoning Herefordshire, become my local landscape, I studied buses on the Isle of Wight (*BY 2002*). Almost everything I wrote then, even including the impending changes, is now out of date.

The dramatic route along the Undercliff between Niton and Ventnor has been severed by drastic land-slips with the buses re-routed like the returning Three Wise Men dodging Herod the King 'by another way'.

The wild experiment with Route Rouge buses, which resulted not infrequently in red buses' straying far from their dedicated routes, has been abandoned, the blue Island Explorer Volvos explore no longer, with the most tragic loss of exploration along the desolate south-west coast along the 'Military Road', and the midi-buses, little as I may have spoken of them in my words, are either dumped or else, in a grand gesture from Southern Vectis, gone out to Ceylon (or should I say Sri Lanka?) or other such places to serve as replacements after the tsunami disaster, except for, I believe, three, two serving as mobile booking offices and the third, painted bright pink with a surplus pot of paint from a previous all-over advert job, converted for

Below: Midi-bus serving as ticket office at the Isle of Wight Rock Festival in 2006. The reason you would be searched (see the notice in the background) was that no glass was allowed on site — a prohibition extended, no doubt, to other 'substances' …

a while for transporting, shamingly for their misdemeanours, the most recalcitrant of Wight delinquents to school; while this was to my mind an entirely praiseworthy effort I do not believe it achieved much success, and the bus seems since, in 'West Wight' livery (still pink), to serve as a reserve.

The booking-office midi-buses served in serious vein at the 2006 IoW Rock Festival, a revival of the famous 1970s event. Now, as then, this required vast SV efforts, including drafting in of 'overseas' buses from associated companies, including, believe it or not, two RMLs — one green, one red. Having walked in excessive heat to survey the traffic *en route* to the site, rather late on its last day, I elected to catch a bus back and thus applied at a midi-bus, senior pass in hand. "I've been waiting for this all weekend!" said the ticket-selling maiden. "This is the first 'senior' I've sold!" It was off a common and entirely unidentified sub-Edmondson-sized roll, numbered merely A 001, and inscribed in biro 'OAP'. I shall always wonder whether she sold many, if any, more …

What I failed to remark upon in my Island article was one of the most classic boobs ever in timetable

publication. First I must state that the Southern Vectis timetables have, until the Go-Ahead takeover, been real gems, filled, apart from sometimes almost incomprehensible details of local services, with all the ferries and with train services onwards, and, with summer issues, cartoons on the covers by the noted comic artist Besley. In one issue, however, a few years ago, there appeared, above an enthusiastic write-up of SV services by a certain Councillor Paul Fuller, a blank frame surrounding the words 'photograph of Paul Fuller'.

I might mention that, by what I must reckon to have been a computer error, my last words in a slightly lugubrious essay on 'Continental Coaches Carrying Cuties' (*BY 2003*) were chopped off. To this you should pencil in, if you have a copy, following the words 'a golden age of', well, of course, 'Continental coach travel'!

Returning to my Island, I must relate that only a few days ago, back from a trip to Bath (qv hereinafter), I boarded a bus in East Cowes and requested a ticket to Niton, my home, requiring a change of bus in Newport, a journey of some 12 miles overall, to which the driver replied "Niton? Bloody hell!" but issued the required ticket. This boldly stated 'The Oxford Bus Company', a bit of a shock to the driver accepting through-bookings on from Newport …

As a senile citizen, I might add, I now have all my bus journeys on the Island for free, of which I take full advantage, and indeed have abandoned my car and its constantly rising costs, while ever lamenting, as described in *BY 2002*, that Vectis fares, ever on the whole increasing, remain, for poor persons who are too young, unreasonably exorbitant.

From here I will return a moment to the earlier stages of the journey which ended with an Oxford ticket. Parental care bade me take my eldest son, undreamed by far more than a dozen years when I first started writing for 'BA' (I am one of those elderly parents considered with some favour in the pages of *The Sunday Times* and other astute publications), to view a potential period of study at the University of Bath (not one of those, even redbrick, which existed when I was in love with Carol!).

This is where I hark back to the subject of articulated buses. He and I travelled up to the University on a splendid 'Bright Orange' articulated Volvo, with many traffic hassles and dramatic right-angle turns in the old streets and a brilliant ascent up monstrous grades to the campus. Even if, in decrepitude, I have largely abandoned the formerly compulsive persuasion of bus photography, I hope that the dear child may win a place there, so that I, when visiting him, may tackle some long-lost delights (*BY 20xx*!).

Left: Recalled to active service 'on hire to Southern Vectis' as a 2006 Rock Festival crowd-mover was this RML, seen negotiating crowd barriers and battlefield metal roadways.

Right: Just as a postscript … nothing to do with the article, save only as an achievement by Robert E. Jowitt in 2006, after decades of effort (albeit decidedly intermittent), successfully to capture a bus in Bridport, Dorset, with the odd-shaped and plumed hill in the background — and without splitting an infinitive, either.

Vanishing independents

ANDREW JAROSZ looks at the rise and fall of independent bus operators in Leeds in the years following deregulation.

All photographs by the author

August 2005 was a milestone in the history of public transport in Leeds. It saw the end of virtually the last independent commercial bus operation — that of Black Prince, a company that had grown and provided competitive bus services for nearly 20 years. With its demise, and the purchase of most of its bus services and vehicles by First, one of England's largest cities was firmly in the hands of FirstGroup, a situation never envisaged by the Transport Act that paved the way for deregulation in 1986. One smaller private operator remained, but its services did not penetrate the heart of the city, and it lasted barely more than a year after Black Prince before its local services were handed over, again to First. Nevertheless, there is a story to be told, a story of numerous private ventures which tried to compete with the big boys, and a story where competition and innovation brought forth numerous interesting buses and entrepreneurs.

Twenty-two years ago the then Conservative Government unlocked a dream — a dream of deregulation and privatisation whereby all local bus services could be operated by any bus company that satisfied competence criteria, and all bus operators that were state-owned or publicly owned would be open to private-sector ownership. There were exceptions, of course; bus services in Northern Ireland would remain regulated, and the sell-off of bus companies was going to take some years, but the eventual dream of politicians was that a lot of local bus companies would compete to provide good local bus services, in a way that the protected local-monopoly companies of 1986 could not.

Unsurprisingly, competition in other metropolitan areas was far more intense and (in cities like Birmingham and Manchester) to a certain extent still exists today. It was always much quieter in Leeds, and one of the obvious barriers to entry was the low-fare policy of West Yorkshire PTA, which had kept fares frozen for five years, and the intense high frequency of its network. There was also an interesting timetable for deregulation, which required operators to commit themselves way in advance of the 26 October 1986

start date. Operators had until 28 February to register their services, which were then published on 1 April. Local councils then had an opportunity to tender for services that were left out, and the whole shooting match stayed in place until January 1987, when modifications could be registered. Also unsurprisingly, the main National Bus Company operators (West Yorkshire Road Car, West Riding Automobile and Yorkshire Woollen District Transport) refused to register in competition with Yorkshire Rider, which was the successor to West Yorkshire PTE buses, all four sticking rigidly to their existing territories and services.

Thus it was that deregulation day brought forth to the streets of Leeds only two new operators, both based in the southern suburb of Morley. One was a partnership of Dennis Muffitt and David Taylor, who, as M&T, operated one route from Morley to Leeds; the other was Black Prince, which registered against both Rider and Yorkshire Woollen — hardly surprising, given that its base was near the boundary between the two companies' territories. Black Prince was to continue through nearly 19 years of intense competition, but others were not nearly as fortunate. Interestingly there was already on the scene a coach operator which had a substantial fleet of contract vehicles but which was never to enter the fray. Independent Coachways of Horsforth operated a large variety of second-hand double-deckers and then built up a substantial fleet of Bristol REs, all for contract work. Following the company's takeover by Thornes of Bubwith the REs gave way to Plaxton-bodied Scania buses acquired from British Airways at Heathrow.

In this chronicle charting the development of competition, operators on the periphery, not actually reaching the centre of Leeds, have been ignored, as have long-distance operations, not often on high frequencies. To these must be added South Yorkshire Road Transport of Pontefract, which remained independent until selling out to West Riding in 1994 and operated with conductors on rear-engined double-deckers well past 1986. Operators such as Lancaster City Transport, Yelloway, Skill's, SUT and East Yorkshire also operated routes into Leeds but rarely carried

Above: Four Seasons served Leeds from 1987 to 1993, when it sold out to West Riding. This Bristol VRT with ECW body had been new to PMT.

passengers within the city. AB Cars of Swillington (with its CVE Omnis) did operate some peak journeys into Leeds from Swillington and Kippax for a short period but concentrated on minibus services around the south-eastern suburbs before having its licences revoked by the Traffic Commissioner in 1990.

Two new operators coming from the east side of the city had to compete with West Riding, and neither fared well. Four Seasons Coaches of Great Preston (set up in 1985) commenced running into Leeds in February 1987 using a Leopard coach on a route later extended to Castleford; routes were expanded with peak-time services from Micklefield and Kippax into Leeds, and double-deckers were later employed, including two Ailsas (acquired from London, but originating with West Midlands), before the company succumbed to competition and sold the services to West Riding in March 1993. The second company was White Rose of Castleford, which in October 1989 took over the Metro Accessbus network from Yorkshire Woollen. This contract only lasted until April 1992, leaving the company to operate competitive services in the Castleford area. It replaced its Leyland Nationals with a collection of double-deckers, including two 'deckers from Four Seasons when that folded, but the

end was to come soon. White Rose signed its own death warrant in December 1994 by acquiring five Iveco-engined Routemasters for both express and stopping services from Castleford to Leeds. While it was quite a sight to see red and white Routemasters in the centre of the city, this venture was never going to stand up economically, and it folded on 6 May 1995, having operated for less than five months.

November 1987 was a significant month for Leeds, with the emergence of four new operators in the city. Yorkshire Rider had surrendered a number of marginal services, and Metro (as West Yorkshire PTE now styled itself) had tendered them out, hoping perhaps to entice new blood. Entice they did, in the shape of Rhodes Coaches, Amberley Coaches, Airebus and Cityline.

Rhodes was the oldest of the companies, having been formed in 1967 and built up a successful coaching business in Yeadon. Its first route was from Bradford to Otley using an L-reg National and a former Grey-Green Leopard, but this was to spawn further operations in the Otley, Yeadon and Rawdon areas, which included services in the north-western corner of Leeds as well as direct commercial routes to and from the city. Vehicles acquired over the years included a new G-reg Leyland Lynx, an East Lancs-bodied Scania, the UK's only Van Hool low-floor bus (an ex demonstrator) and an ECW-bodied Olympian coach.

Amberley was formed in 1982, taking vehicles from the Sidney Tales fleet, and was based at Amberley Road in north-east Leeds. By 1987 the operation was

Above: At the end of 1994 White Rose purchased five AEC Routemasters for services between Castleford and Leeds. These were smartly turned out but would be short-lived: White Rose ceased trading in May 1995.

Below: An old-established coach operator, Rhodes started running buses in Leeds in 1987. Its fleet included both new and used vehicles, one of the more unusual used examples being this long-wheelbase Leyland Olympian with ECW body, which had been new to London Country for Green Line services.

Above: Amberley started a service between Pudsey and Leeds in 1987. Its fleet included Leyland Nationals; this bus had started life with Crosville.

in the hands of Barry Walker, one of the original partners, and moved to Troydale Mills at Pudsey. Amberley started with the X88 from Pudsey to Leeds using a Leyland National and a Plaxton-bodied RE coach which originated with Crosville. By the end of 1988 four Nationals were owned, and in the following year a DMS from Graham's of Paisley heralded a stream of double-deckers, some of which were resold, as the company also operated as a dealer on the side. Its operations remained largely on the Pudsey corridor but were subsequently extended towards Bradford and east Leeds.

Airebus was a new operation set up by Sheffield-based SUT, owned by Tony Lavin's ATL group, which also bought Yelloway and Crosville. SUT had set up a competitive operation in Sheffield during 1987 using second-hand Nationals and Bristol VRs and took over a group of tendered services focused on Pudsey, for which a base was established at a dealer on the Grangefield Trading Estate. Nine DMS Fleetlines in a livery of bright blue and cream were acquired for the job, but these were soon supplemented by Nationals as they moved back and forth between Sheffield and Leeds. The following year these were replaced by ex-Lothian Atlanteans, which operated in both cities in SUT's dark-red colour scheme, and operations expanded with the capture of more contracts, which took some services outside the city. In 1989 Airebus moved to a more central facility in Kirkstall,

appropriately next to the river Aire, and then at the end of April the company ceased trading. This was just part of a much greater scenario which involved the dismantling of the ATL group: Crosville was sold to PMT, while SUT ended up with South Yorkshire Transport, as did the Sheffield-based operations of West Riding in October of the same year; National Express Group was also involved in taking over parts of the ATL empire, and the Kirkstall depot was to pass to Yorkshire Voyager, a NatEx joint venture which had taken over express-coach operation from the West Yorkshire Road Car Co.

Cityline, with only five vehicles, took over one route through Wortley to Pudsey but was clearly feared by Yorkshire Rider because it was a new operation set up by PMT, based in Stoke-on-Trent. PMT Commercial Director Steve Ellis knew the area well, having studied at Leeds University, and had previously managed West Riding's Castleford depot, so it came as no surprise when Yorkshire Rider obtained a High Court injunction preventing Ellis from using the Red Rider name already being used at Moreton, on the Wirral. A Bristol LHS, two VRs and a pair of new Dodge minibuses were stationed at Elland Road, but the potential was never realised, and the operation closed a year later,

at the end of October 1988. With hindsight, had PMT ever become a competitive force in Leeds this would surely have been eliminated in March 1994, when Badgerline took over Rider, having already acquired PMT a few months earlier!

Returning to the Morley operations, the two incumbent independents were joined in January 1988 by Roy Wilcox, trading as Roy's of Morley, on a short-lived commercial service. A coach operator since 1982, its only bus was a Leyland National (acquired from Taff Ely) which had previously operated a tendered service around Cleckheaton and Heckmondwike. Both the bus and the Leeds service passed to Amberley in December of that year, Roy's concentrating thereafter on coaching.

M&T, which in 1987 acquired a flat-front Bristol RE from Cambus, continued with its two-vehicle operation until February 1989, when the partners went their separate ways. After the split Dennis Muffitt continued on the 46 route as Miramare Coaches, using Leyland Nationals and a Fleetline, until closure in November 1996. David Taylor, on the other hand, embraced double-deck operation and built up a fleet of VR, Fleetline and Ailsa double-deckers, peaking at 13 in 1994. By now known as Taylors Coaches and using an all-over red livery, the company moved in 1992 to Whitehall Road and built up a network of cross-city services in a similar manner to Black Prince — to the point when Black Prince painted two vehicles in an

identical livery, because competition, particularly for stand space on Vicar Lane was fierce.

Black Prince had been founded by Brian Crowther in 1969 and undertook a range of coach and contract operations until 1986. Its attractive green livery was replaced for buses by red and yellow, the combination of the two colours varying from bus to bus. The company started off with four routes on deregulation day and used ex-GM Buses Atlanteans and Bristol REs from various sources.

Although the company wasn't looking for confrontation with Rider in 1986, it soon became clear that the larger operator was going to try to snuff out any opposition at birth. By 1987 the gloves were off: Rider was running 12 minibuses against Prince, as well as extra buses, and was indulging in stand-blocking and driver-poaching. To be fair to Rider, it became paranoid, believing that it would be attacked by BET minibuses in the way that Bee Line Buzz had settled in Manchester, and thus Rider accumulated the UK's largest fleet of nearly 400 minibuses. When the attack failed to materialise, the minis were turned to other competitive uses.

Progressively Black Prince opened up new cross-city routes, and the majority of work became commercial. A depot in Gildersome was opened, and, in spite of competitive attacks, the fleet grew to over 60 vehicles. In its early days as a commercial operator the company majored on the Volvo Ailsa and by the mid-

1990s would own nearly 40, making it by this time the largest fleet of the type in the country. Perhaps the most interesting was the experimental twin-staircase B55 built for London Transport (V3), acquired in 1992 after a rollover accident; this became a long-term restoration project and would finally enter service some 12 years later, long after all the other Ailsas had gone.

January 1990 saw a first foray into bus work by AJC Coaches. Originally set up as Fallas Coaches, the company had been acquired by Arthur Carrick, who in 1994 passed it on to Ken Beardsley, who renamed the bus operation as Angloblue. Having started off in a small way on tendered services, it made its big commercial push in 1992 with the introduction of the Beeston service. After Tigers, Leopards and a Bristol LH, Nationals started arriving around 1994, an ex-Rider example (which came from Liverpool) and an ex-demonstrator National 2 being notable amongst the 15-strong fleet. Operations ended abruptly in September 1996, all routes and some buses passing to Rider in exchange for the latter's Gold Rider coach operation and five coaches. AJC continued as a coach operator for a few more years before going bankrupt.

An interesting new commercial operator came on the scene in February 1992, started by former York City & District manager Nigel Jolliffe. Ten ex-Ribble Nationals, based at Hunslet Forge, formed the opening fleet of Quickstep Travel, the vehicles being painted in an attractive livery of cream and red with a logo of top hat and cane. Jolliffe had been a member of Harry Blundred's buy-out crew at Devon General in 1986, so it was not hard to trace the inspiration for the livery.

Quickstep started commercial operation straight away, and the fleet was up to 20 in just over 12 months, by which time about eight cross-city routes were being operated. It ordered some new Ikarus-bodied DAF SB220s, but in November 1993 it was purchased by Rider. The attractive livery was retained until the Leeds City Link re-branding in 1995, but Quickstep was to survive as a low-cost subsidiary until 2006. Various vehicles, including Atlanteans, Metrobuses and minibuses, were transferred from the main fleet, and the unit continued to hold its own operating licence whilst based at Kirkstall Road depot.

The next significant year was 1994. Yorkshire Rider sold out to Badgerline in March, Rhodes sold out to Rider in April, Amberley ceased operations in May, and Taylor sold out to K Line of Huddersfield in August. Virtually all of Rhodes' vehicles passed to Rider in a deal reputedly worth seven figures; some were transferred to Quickstep, others moving on to South

Below: Taylor's Coaches built up a fleet of red-liveried double-deckers of various types, including this former West Midlands PTE Alexander-bodied Ailsa acquired from London Buses.

Above: AJC Coaches started running local services in 1990. Its fleet included this comparatively rare Leyland Tiger with ECW body, which had originally been a Green Line coach.

Below: Angloblue operated in Leeds in the mid-1990s. Its fleet included this 10.6m Leyland National 2, which had been new in 1980 to West Yorkshire Road Car. The company's bus operations were taken over by Yorkshire Rider in 1996.

Right: In 1992 Quickstep appeared in Leeds, quickly building up a fleet of 20 vehicles which included this Ikarus-bodied DAF SB220. The business was acquired by Yorkshire Rider in 1993 — and survived as a subsidiary until 2006.

Wales Transport, and Rhodes remained a small coaching company (probably for tax reasons) until selling out its one-vehicle operation to Kevin Jackson a few years later. Amberley sold its Bradford route to Black Prince, which used a blue livery both to maintain a link with Amberley and to rekindle memories of Samuel Ledgard, who had operated the route in years gone by. Taylor sold 12 double-deckers to K Line, but the company soon announced its intention to replace them all with new DAF/Ikarus saloons, of which nine examples duly arrived.

Mention must also be made of Ken-Dell Buses, which operated for less than three months in 1995 on a route between Hunslet and Middleton with a 14-seat Ford Transit, and Godsons Coaches, which won the two airport contracts from Metro in 1995 with two new DAF/Ikarus buses but lost them three years later.

Bigfoot Buses was another enterprise to run for less than three years but which gave Rider plenty of competition. Set up by Geldards Coaches in November 1995, Bigfoot started with five Nationals operating from Bramley and Owlcotes to the city and then up to Holt Park. During 1996 more routes were added, and another four Nationals and numerous DAF SB220s arrived. Also purchased was a new Scania L113 single-decker with East Lancs Flyte bodywork, but this was sold to Black Prince in April 1998 (and still operates for First in Leeds today). Bigfoot closed down in September 1998, some of the buses and routes passing to Taylors, but Geldards has since gone from strength to strength and today operates the largest fleet of yellow double-deck school buses in the county, as well as running occasional commercial services to music festivals and a tendered leisure-bus operation for Metro.

One more independent operation threatened for a short period but lasted only two years. Having initially taken over a tendered service, two coach operators based in Horsforth — Hunters and J&B —set up Optional Bus. The opening fleet comprised Nationals that had come straight from London Country South West, and the new operator adopted its colourful green livery as standard. As routes expanded, more Nationals and Atlanteans (with Park Royal and Roe bodies) were acquired until three routes requiring 13 buses were operated commercially. Nationals, Metroriders and a VR purchased from other sources adopted the LCSW-inspired livery. In August 1999 Optional's routes and eight buses were sold to Rider, but the two coach operators that formed it remain independent, running yellow double-deckers on school services.

The withdrawal of Optional Bus left just Taylors and Black Prince operating competitive services around the city, but events were unfolding which were to interest the Office of Fair Trading and the Competition Commission.

In January 2000 it was announced that Arriva (which had by then taken over the Yorkshire Bus Group, owner of West Riding and Yorkshire Woollen) was taking a partial stake in the K Line group, and it soon emerged that this meant the acquisition of the Taylors operation and the depot in Leeds, the Honley (Huddersfield) operations remaining with K Line. In April Arriva took over 23 single-deck buses comprising 18 DAF/Ikarus, two DAF/Optare and three Darts, and there began a gradual run-down of services, culminating in the closure of the Leeds depot in January 2001, leaving just one Leeds route to be worked from Wakefield. This unprecedented retreat

Above: In 1994 Taylor's bus operations were sold to K-Line, which modernised the fleet by introducing nine DAF SB220s with 49-seat Ikarus bodywork.

Below: Between 1995 and 1998 Bigfoot provided competition for Yorkshire Rider, using mainly Leyland Nationals. This vehicle was new to Crosville.

Right: Optional Bus operated for two years using a livery inspired by London Country South West, as seen on a one-time London Country Leyland Atlantean with Roe body in Pudsey. The company sold its routes and eight buses to Yorkshire Rider in 1999.

closure of Rider's Kinsley depot in 1997 and the handover of its Wakefield routes to Arriva after 20 years of operation, reached the attention of the OFT. In 2000 the Competition Commission raided the offices of Arriva and First (which by then owned Rider) and eventually concluded that there had been anti-competitive collusion. First turned 'State's evidence' and escaped financial penalty, but Arriva was fined more than £200,000. However, the clock was never turned back, and Black Prince was left on its own to battle the might of First.

Only one other operator emerged during the 20th century. In January 2000 Aztecbird of Guiseley — a reincarnation of an earlier coach operator — started a Rural Bus Grant-sponsored route from Otley to Menston station. It developed other commercial and tendered routes in the Otley/Ilkley region, but its only contribution to the bus scene in central Leeds was winning the 757 airport route (in October 2001), which was extended to Otley. Two Csepel-bodied Neoplans bought for this route were later replaced by two Ikarus Polaris-bodied DAFs, but the contract was lost three years later, and the company went under in November 2004. A new operator, Pegasus.com, was set up to take on some of its service work, but this also folded, in November 2006.

The Black Prince fleet peaked at around 60 vehicles in 1995, which year marked a return to Fountain Street depot in Morley, but a public inquiry, coupled with a serious illness suffered by Brian Crowther, forced a reduction to around 40 vehicles working the most profitable routes. Routemasters had operated for a while on the intense Headingley corridor, but Scanias were preferred for long-term reliability. New buses,

in the shape of MAN/Optare Vectas, East Lancs-bodied Scanias and MetroRiders, were purchased, and a subsidiary — Leeds Suburban Buses, using a version of the former Leeds City Transport livery and fleetname — was introduced.

By 2001 Black Prince was on its own, and the writing was on the wall. Good drivers were hard to find, insurance costs were rising exponentially, First was using cheap day tickets to build up customer loyalty, and there was a general decline in passenger numbers. It came as no surprise to learn subsequently that First, Black Prince and the OFT had been in talks for three years before Crowther finally hung up his gloves. Ultimately First did not buy the company but took over most of the service registrations, most of the Scania buses and a lot of spares, as well as taking on most of the staff. Routes were reorganised, but, perhaps not surprisingly, nobody stepped in to pick up the discarded service registrations.

The experience of the past 20 years has shown that no small private operator can withstand the might of the large national groups that now dominate our local bus services. Some operators failed through lack of ambition, some failed through their own incompetence, some were obviously set up to sell out as soon as they became worth something to the opposition, some sold out when they were made an offer they couldn't refuse, some sold out when they were on the verge of collapse, and some *possibly* closed down, when it was worth their while to do so. To Black Prince — a target from day one but which tried hard to gain the critical mass necessary to survive — must go the credit for running a professional operation for nearly 20 years. There will never be another operator like it.

Above: Aztecbird secured the contract to run the service from Leeds to Leeds/Bradford Airport and on to Otley in 2001, and for this it initially used two rare Csepel-bodied Neoplans, one of which is seen at the railway station in Leeds. Aztecbird lost the contract in 2004.

Below: Black Prince was the longest-lived of the independent operators serving Leeds in the post-deregulation period and operated an interesting and varied fleet. This Mercedes-Benz O.405/Optare Prisma was purchased new in 1996.

Above: Black Prince had a fondness for Scanias, and this bus, seen in Pudsey, was one of a number of second-hand Scania double-deckers operated by the company. It had been new to Greater Manchester Transport and was acquired from the Stagecoach-owned GM Buses South operation. Northern Counties built the body.

Below: The Black Prince fleet also featured Ailsas, including this bus which started life with London Buses and had two doors and two staircases — note the blank panel covering the staircase at the rear of the lower deck. When acquired by Black Prince it had suffered accident damage, and 12 years passed before it actually ran in Leeds.

The melody lingers on

Buses can last many years, and a lot of those on the road at any given time have long since gone out of production. **PETER ROWLANDS** reflects on this time-warp characteristic of the industry.

All photographs by Peter Rowland

You know the buses in your own town or city, don't you? You know what they look like, clustered together; how they sum up a familiar environment. They're part of the character of the place, aren't they? Its lifeblood, almost. They form the backdrop to your everyday experience. Even in this era of uniform bus-group liveries the combination of body types, chassis makes and operators in any specific place is still likely to be pretty distinctive.

But how often do you consider that a lot of the buses in question are no longer in production? That some, in fact, were dropped by their builders years ago, and that those builders might not even exist any more?

Buses aren't like cars, which are mostly built by companies that keep on turning out vehicles somewhere

in the world. Buses get ordered, get built and go into service; the world turns; life moves on. Don't ask for a repeat performance — it may not be an option.

Yet vehicles built by defunct manufacturers or based on discontinued designs simply soldier on, sometimes for years afterwards. They're in constant public view — a monument to the past, and a reminder of how someone hoped the future would look.

Everyone discovering the bus world probably goes through a similar cycle of observation and enlightenment … and in some cases disappointment over all the might-have-beens.

Having grown up in Newcastle, where open-platform double-deckers had pretty much vanished by the late 1960s, I was amazed to encounter thousands still in

Left: When the author discovered provincial front-engined buses still in service in the 1970s production had long since ceased. Changes in public funding for new buses meant only one-man models were on offer. But this Massey-bodied Leyland Titan, delivered new to Wigan Corporation, was still in service with Greater Manchester when photographed in Wigan in April 1981.

operation in other towns and cities well into the 1970s. But no one was building them any more; by the time I became aware of them they were all relics of the past.

I have a sense that in between the two world wars people probably felt something like this in relation to the many open-staircase buses then still in service. You often see them in photographs and snatches of film from the 1930s, running alongside later, enclosed-body counterparts. They were common enough, but the whole concept of travelling 'inside' or 'on top' was by then outmoded, and in a sense those buses already represented a bygone age.

A similar thing happens now. For instance, you'd find it impossible to buy a high-floor double-decker now; yet thousands of high-floor examples are still happily running on Britain's streets: buses as they used to be.

All in all, I bet you that at least half the buses in service in the fleet where you live now are not in production any more, if you take account of both bodies and chassis.

Even recent, low-floor models didn't necessarily stay in production for long. How many President double-deck bodies from Northern Counties/Plaxton have you seen in service lately? Dozens, probably. Yet the name of the builder, Northern Counties, was abandoned in 1999, and the Wigan factory itself was closed in 2005. Plaxton has since been reborn, but has no connection with the plant that built those bodies.

In its final years Northern Counties was owned by TransBus, the parent of former rival bodybuilder Alexander; but Alexander's comparable ALX400 double-decker is now also effectively a body of the past, replaced by the Enviro400, the futuristic body from Alexander Dennis (the reborn company that emerged when TransBus failed).

Below: By the time this Volvo B7TL was photographed in May 2003 the Northern Counties bodywork factory in Wigan was just two years from closure. Both body and chassis have now been replaced by later models, but this bus probably has at least a dozen years' more life in it.

Of the double-deck bodies on the road in large numbers today only Wright's Eclipse Gemini is still available in 2007. Moreover, the Volvo B7TL chassis on which the majority are based has been replaced by the B9TL.

It's partly the relentless pace of change that transforms many bus fleets quite quickly into tantalising collections of discontinued models; but there are other factors at work here too.

For one thing, buses last a long time — 10 years, conservatively, and sometimes twice that figure (or even longer). A car is old at seven years, when a bus is barely past its prime. A lot can happen in seven years, especially in the volatile world of passenger transport, where orders come fitfully at best. It's constant feast and famine for many bus builders, and sometimes they can't stay the course. So their creations often have to survive long after they've vanished.

In the past, to some extent bus builders tried to anticipate changes in fashion by designing conservatively. That's why, for instance, the boxy, standard-style double-deck bodies by Northern

Above: Alexander's ALX400 body has become a modern classic and is likely to be seen on our streets for years to come, but the design has now been replaced by the Enviro400. In the early 2000s Travel West Midlands introduced differentiated liveries for its various operations, including the two-tone blue and white seen on this ALX400-bodied Volvo in the Travel Coventry fleet in June 2003.

Above right: Seen in Putney en route from Wandsworth to Richmond in August 2006, this Volvo B7TL shows the bodybuilder's name as TransBus, a company that had by then disappeared. It lives on as Alexander Dennis, although the ALX400 body has since been replaced.

Right: Of the double-deck bus designs seen widely in London in 2007, only Wrights' Eclipse Gemini body remains available, and even this has been revised. The example here, on a Volvo chassis, is seen in Fulham in July 2005, on the day low-floor buses replaced Routemasters on the 22.

Counties/Park Royal/Roe/MCW survived for more than 20 years. Operators don't want to stock new collections of spare parts, and manufacturers don't want the expense of designing new products that might have only a very short production life.

This means that in the past, discontinued buses didn't necessarily *appear* all that old. Their replacements may not have been radically different from what went before. Yet details changed as the years passed, and inevitably the older models eventually became fixed in a kind of time-warp representing the era in which they were built.

The less charitable might observe that Eastern Coach Works' Bristol VR double-deck body already looked outmoded from the day the first one appeared. It was, after all, based on a design with roots back in the 1940s. Be that as it may, it stayed in production in gradually evolving form from 1968 to 1981, and, in fairness, it arguably comes closest to representing true continuity of design and form in postwar years.

Nevertheless, the Bristol factory that built those VR chassis was closed by its then owner, Leyland, in 1983, and the ECW body factory lasted only a few years longer. After the VR was dropped it started building a new body design for the Leyland Olympian, but then the plant was closed amid political and financial wrangling about the future shape of the industry.

Yet Bristol VRs still struggle on in a few fleets as I write this in early 2007 — 26 years after production

Above: **The Park Royal/Roe double-deck body design of the early 1970s was one of the precursors of the bus industry's 'standard' look of the 1970s and 1980s. This example, originally in the London Country fleet, is seen in Croydon in 1990 in the livery of London & Country, the company formed from London Country's south-western operations.**

ceased. Orphaned, you might say, and reflecting a remarkably distant past in terms of how buses should look.

Sometimes manufacturers exaggerate the time-warp effect by producing models that are conceived to reflect someone's unique vision (usually the operator's) of a different way of doing things. You can see some classic examples of this among the double-deck bodies built in the 1960s and early 1970s. Alongside the routine designs of the major builders emerged some striking customer-inspired designs.

For instance, there were the unmistakable 'Mancunian' double-deck bodies built for Manchester between 1968 and 1972 on Leyland Atlantean and Daimler Fleetline chassis, with their massive, square-cornered bodies and deep, idiosyncratic windscreens. The first time I saw one, in the early 1970s, I thought it was one of the best-looking bus bodies I'd ever encountered; but by then the design had already been dropped. The windscreens had been found too heavy

Right: The Eastern Coach Works design that had evolved into this 1977 body on a Bristol VRT of Lincolnshire Road Car can be traced back directly to bodywork on wartime Bristol K chassis. It is seen in Lincoln in August 1990, nine years after VR production came to an end.

Left: This unmistakable deep windscreen was one of the trademark features of the Mancunian body, as was the translucent roof. This MCW-bodied Atlantean is seen in Ashton in August 1981, nine years after the design was dropped.

and expensive to replace, and it was inconvenient to operate models that had no true equivalent elsewhere. Yet Mancunians continued to run in Manchester right up to 1984.

Though they were less celebrated, Leeds also had distinctive Roe double-deck bodies in that era, again built on long-wheelbase Atlantean and Fleetline chassis, and equipped with panoramic side windows and unique front mouldings. In both cases these buses became synonymous with the cities in which they operated, yet in both cases they were only actually in production for a few short years.

If you want to talk seriously idiosyncratic, of course, you need only switch your gaze to Nottingham, where the municipal operator continued to specify unique double-deck body designs long after other operators had decided such an approach was simply too expensive. Whether they were Atlanteans or Fleetlines, or later underfloor-engined Leylands and Volvos, they had a whole array of features that differed from practice elsewhere. Most conspicuously, these included the trademark inward-sloping panel for the front destination screen, which arguably gave the whole vehicle an ungainly, top-heavy look; but over the years there were other unusual features too. These variously included a very narrow front entrance, a very deep cut-away over the rear engine compartment, and repeater rear light clusters in unfamiliar positions.

I suppose in their day these buses rather defied the theory that idiosyncrasy tends to be short-lived; the

Left: Shallow panoramic windows and angular front mouldings defined the distinctive Leeds look of this Roe design on an Atlantean chassis, though production was short-lived. This one is seen in 1979.

Left: For many years Nottingham's buses were distinctive for their unique, top-heavy look, demonstrated by this example by Northern Counties from the 1980-2 batch of Leyland Atlanteans, which was shared with East Lancs. It was photographed nearing the end of its life in August 1998 — 10 years after Leyland was bought by Volvo, and the year before the Northern Counties name vanished forever. Atlantean production had ceased 12 years earlier, in 1986.

Nottingham design kept appearing and evolving over several decades. However, by the 1990s the operator had reined in its enthusiasm for its one-off designs, and started buying more standard-looking vehicles at last. But those that were in service at that point ran on for at least another 10 years — a tribute to the adventurous spirit of those who gave birth to them.

It's not always operators that initiate singular designs. Manufacturers themselves sometimes go out on a limb and create products with unique characteristics. Not that this brings them any greater guarantee of survival.

One of the most bizarre sagas in this respect is that of the Dartline single-deck body, with its bold curving windscreen, which was developed by Duple in 1988 for the then-new Dennis Dart. This must be one of the few

bus bodies with the distinction of having been produced by three different bodybuilders during its relatively short life: Duple until that company's closure in 1989, then Carlyle until its closure in 1992, then Marshall, which first redesigned it as the C36 before replacing it with a new body for the low-floor Dart SLF.

Marshall, incidentally, defies easy categorisation in terms of its market presence. Several times over a number of decades the parent group withdrew from the bus market, then clawed back a presence for itself, before finally selling the business to a management buyout in 2001. (It failed a year later.) Yet many of its products are still in service as I write — even some of those striking Dartline bodies.

Willowbrook is another long-standing builder that didn't disappear with a big bang but somehow just

Top: When parts of Duple's business were acquired by Plaxton in 1989 rights to its Dartline body design were sold to Carlyle, which had emerged from the maintenance operations of the old Midland Red Omnibus Co. Carlyle supplied a small batch to Rossendale Transport — which does survive today, even though both Duple and Carlyle are just memories. This bus is seen at Haslingden in 1990.

Above: When Carlyle failed in 1992 the rights to the Dartline body were acquired by Marshall, which went on to redesign it with this more substantial front bumper assembly; this was meant to offer more protection for the vulnerable windscreen than did the original, though arguably it sacrificed the finesse. This Dart is seen in Oxford in 1995.

Left: In the late 1990s Marshall replaced the compromised Dartline styling with a new, more coherent design for low-floor Dennis and MAN chassis. This Dart is seen in Enfield in July 1999. The Marshall name finally disappeared from the industry in 2002, but many of these vehicles are still in front-line service.

Right: Marshall dipped in and out of the bus market over many years but built few double-deck bodies. Newport Borough Council took a batch on Scania chassis, including this one, seen in February 1990.

faded away. In the 1970s and early 1980s it built double-deck bodies in quite large numbers to a variety of different styles — some designed in-house, some copies of other manufacturers' products. Then its order book simply dried up. Yet it stuttered back into action five years later with a range of workmanlike single-deck bodies.

Another manufacturer that struck a highly distinctive design note in its latter days was Leyland, whose Lynx single-decker was notable for its sharply raked driver's windscreen. It was built in modest numbers from 1986, but when Leyland was bought by Volvo in 1988 the future of the model was thrown into doubt, and it was eventually dropped in 1992. Yet for the best part of the

next 15 years those Lynxes remained a common sight in many of Britain's cities, a unique and very visible reminder of the disappearance of their iconic manufacturer.

You could say the same applies to Leyland's Olympian double-decker, but in this case Volvo continued producing it for years after the Leyland takeover. In fact it was dropped only in 2000 and spiritually lived on in the low-floor B7TL. So a degree of continuity was maintained.

Not so with the MCW Metrobus double-decker, whose evolution more or less ended when its Laird Group parent simply gave up on the bus industry in 1989. The chassis design passed to the organisation

Above: Willowbrook stopped building double-deck bodies in the early 1980s, but this Cardiff example, based loosely on rival bodybuilders' standard designs of the period, was among a batch supplied on Bristol VRT chassis in 1977. Photographed in 1989, by which time Willowbrook's reincarnation as a low-cost single-deck producer was coming to an end, it was scrapped two years later.

Below: The Leyland Lynx was distinctive with its square profile and backwards-tilting driver's windscreen. Seen when less than a year old, in July 1989, this example in the Cardiff fleet was still running in the city 10 years later — seven years after the model was dropped by Volvo.

Right: When Volvo acquired Leyland in 1989 it initially seemed excited about gaining the Lynx single-deck design and indeed went on to launch a Mk II version, with distinctive protruding radiator moulding. But by the time this smart Halton Borough Transport example was photographed in August 1995 the model had already been out of production for three years.

Left: The boxy Manchester 'Standard' look was developed originally for Leyland Atlantean and Daimler Fleetline chassis and was later also used on Leyland Olympians and Dennis Dominators, but when it appeared on a batch of Metrobuses — the first to be bodied by Northern Counties — it aroused wide interest. This one is seen at Stockport when new in the summer of 1986. Metrobus production ended three years afterwards, but this bus lasted nearly 20.

Right: Routemasters were in production for only nine years, from 1959 to 1968, but this one was still in service with the Stagecoach group when photographed in the City 31 years later.

then known as DAF Bus and the body to Optare, but production of its reinvented successor ran to only a fraction of the numbers of the Metrobus in its heyday, and links with the original became increasingly difficult to spot. Yet for years afterwards Metrobuses were the mainstay of various large bus fleets, notably in London and Birmingham; and there are still Metrobuses around in 2007. There can be few more telling examples of a bus that was consigned to history just when it was becoming accepted as a true standard.

Except, of course, for one: the Routemaster. This was in production for just nine years, from 1959 to 1968, yet the London fleet ran on for a mind-bending 37 years after that. Such an extraordinary life span is hard now to believe. Yet chassis builder AEC stopped producing double-deckers in the same year it built the last Routemaster, and the AEC brand name was dropped in 1977. The factory closed two years later, as did that of bodybuilder Park Royal; and Leyland, the parent of both, was acquired by Volvo in 1988. So you could say the Routemaster was obsolete the day the last one rolled off the line, and was well and truly orphaned for the last 17 years of its life.

And what of today? Well, there's currently even less standardisation than before among bus models,

certainly between one manufacturer and another. Competition for consumer appeal has finally emerged as a significant factor in bus design, and manufacturers want to build buses that operators will be able to 'sell' to passengers. Naturally they tend to have different ideas about how to do this.

At the same time, the big bus groups are not so much dominated as in the past by engineers, who felt they needed to put a unique stamp on their products. The manufacturers now tend to hold more sway.

All of which means that these days you can get buses with a wide range of different appearances and features to do the same job. This certainly brings variety to the bus world, but it also means that some of those designs are likely to have a fairly short life. So in the future, as in the present, the bus world looks like continuing to be one based on past ideas of how things should be done.

Perhaps things can never be any other way.

Below: The future? An Alexander Dennis Enviro400 seen in Putney in August 2006, soon after entering service with London General. At the time of writing it is one of the few double-deck designs currently in service that you could actually go out and order.

Desert-island 'deckers

If you were to be stranded on a desert island with limited transport facilities, which eight double-deckers would you like to have operating there? **JOHN BURNETT** offers his choice.

1. Northern General Routemaster

Left: The best of the best. Tailored to its role as a medium-distance trunk-service vehicle, the forward-entrance 30-footer was regarded by many as the best version of this wonderful machine. Fifty were bought new plus LT's only example of this configuration (RMF1254), which was instantly recognisable as the only Northern Routemaster with opening upper-deck front windows. A preserved example is seen at the MetroCentre Rally in 1996, showing the original dark-red livery.

2. Newcastle trolleybus

Below: Trolleybuses have a unique attraction; there is an indefinable 'rightness' to the way they do things, the absolute silence when stationary and quiet power when on the move. For many travelling south from Scotland to the North of England the overhead at Gosforth terminus gave the feeling of being almost at journey's end. Six-wheelers were the most appealing; this is one of the Northern Coachbuilders-bodied Sunbeam S7s, which formed part of the complete renewal of the Newcastle Corporation trolleybus fleet in the immediate postwar years.

3. Edinburgh Corporation Daimler CVG6

Above: At a time of new-vehicle shortages following World War 2 Edinburgh Corporation purchased 72 Metro-Cammell-bodied Daimlers, mostly CVG6 models but also some CVD6s, with bodies to the design of Birmingham Corporation. This body style was essentially prewar, and these vehicles seemed incredibly antiquated by the time the last one was withdrawn in 1968. At that time there was a transport museum in Edinburgh, and one survivor served as an exhibit there until the museum's closure; still owned by City of Edinburgh Council it now resides at the Scottish Vintage Bus Museum at Lathalmond.

4. Midland Red D9

Below: At a time when the UK no longer builds very many of its own buses it is difficult to comprehend how, not so very long ago, there were operators that built their own vehicles. The last double-decker to be designed and put into production by Midland Red was the D9, an advanced-specification integral vehicle with independent front suspension. By the time the underfloor-engined D10 was developed the company's policy had changed, and Daimler Fleetlines became the standard for the fleet.

5. Bournemouth Sunbeam MF2B

Above: Between 1958 and 1962 Bournemouth Corporation purchased 40 Weymann-bodied Sunbeam MF2Bs, the final group of which were the last new trolleybuses built for the British market. These were much more elegant vehicles than the Atlanteans and Fleetlines that were entering service during the same period, and it was sad that the trolleys had such short lives; all were gone by 1969.

6. Ex-London Transport RTL

Below: After the war London Transport, like every other bus operator, had a desperate need for new buses. AEC could not meet this need on its own, and Leyland built a version of its Titan chassis to an LT specification which made it possible to swap bodies with the RT-class AEC Regents. Falling passenger numbers in the 1950s brought about premature withdrawals of both RTs and RTLs. Many operators, particularly independents, snapped these buses up and had many years of good service from them. This is one of a batch of RTLs that replaced ancient petrol-engined Titans in Jersey.

7. Bristol Lodekka LD

Right: The Bristol Lodekka was a great leap forward in bus design, combining the convenience of the highbridge bus with the operational versatility of the lowbridge double-decker. The LD is a great bus to drive and has a distinctly vintage feel, with a gearbox which requires double-declutching, vacuum brakes which need a firm push to slow the bus, and precise steering without the complication of power assistance. Eastern Scottish continued to specify the LD after the air-braked FS became available.

8. AEC Bridgemaster

Below: Seen by some as the unfortunate offspring of a marriage between a Routemaster and a Lodekka, the Bridgemaster was not one of AEC's sales successes. Many operators had a need for low-height double-deckers, but the Lodekka was not available on the open market, so AEC had an opportunity to satisfy this demand. Development was slow, however, and not enough customers came back for more. By the time production ceased in 1962 fewer than 200 had been built in six years of production. East Yorkshire was one of the biggest buyers of the type, taking both rear- and forward-entrance variants. Note the inward-sloping upper-deck pillars, designed to clear the North Bar at Beverley.

The image problem

Buses suffer from a downmarket image, argues **DAVID THROWER**. Can that be changed?

Buses continue to receive what most theatre critics might describe as mixed reviews. Readers of this publication, by definition, will be enthusiasts. And enthusiasts seriously like buses, whether they take the form of the latest high-tech model, perhaps powered by anything from solar panels to chicken-manure (I exaggerate, but only slightly), or some rather tired and down-at-heel VR looking as though it desperately needs a sympathetic preservationist. All are worthy of interest, and perhaps even worth a photograph.

Passenger perceptions are naturally very different indeed, diametrically opposed even, from those of enthusiasts. All too often the users' perceptions — and almost all users are emphatically *not* enthusiasts — are of an inferior product. Unreliable, expensive, dirty, inconvenient. We constantly need to remind ourselves of that fact, even if it doesn't accurately fit our own experience of some of the better operators around.

In a golden age, now long gone, buses were often seen by the public as a largely well-run industry. Standardised fleets, often municipally owned, in smart liveries, operating out of solidly built garages, ran regular and (mostly) punctual services, watched over by rather

Left: **Was this the Golden Age? A Midland Red FEDD in Leicester in 1955 — a time when buses allegedly ran with almost military efficiency, but when little thought was given to marketing.** Michael H. C. Baker collection

Right: **The bus industry is justifiably proud of its heritage, as demonstrated by an Arriva Dennis Dart in Llandudno wearing a 1950s-style Crosville livery. When Crosville buses were painted like this car ownership was low, and bus operators had a captive market for their services.** Stewart J. Brown

Right: UK North came to the end of the road in 2006 after a high-profile 'bus war' in Manchester which helped bring the city centre to a standstill when streets and bus stands could not cope with the volume of buses. This is a Volvo Olympian with East Lancs body. *Stewart J. Brown*

forbidding inspectors who would have Something To Say back at the garage if a bus ran early or late.

Back in the 1950s, when labour was plentiful and cheap, there was almost military pride and discipline, and many companies were prime symbols of local or even regional identity. One has only to think of names such as Alexander, Edinburgh Corporation, United Automobile, Midland Red, Western Welsh, Southdown or Aldershot & District to recall those days.

That era ended in the 1960s and 1970s with staff shortages, industrial unrest, anæmic liveries and a precipitate decline in use due to the huge growth in private motoring. It was perhaps the Bus & Coach Council's 'The Future of the Bus' report of 1982 that sounded the first real alarm at the way bus travel seemed to be sliding gracefully towards ultimate near-extinction. 'We'd All Miss The Bus', read the well-remembered poster supporting the BCC's campaign.

The next two decades saw deregulation and a further continuing slide in passenger numbers in most of Britain's big cities but very sharp growth in London from the late 1990s and varying degrees of decline, stabilisation or modest growth in smaller towns and rural counties and regions.

Unfashionable

In many ways the new century has in policy terms come to the rescue of bus travel. A succession of reports has warned of the economic and human effects of climate change and, implicitly, the need for much better public transport. But, at the same time, bus travel remains, shall we say, unfashionable with the Motoring Masses, and unpopular with many users. In a world dominated by marketing imagery it's not cool to be seen waiting at a bus stop.

And an upgraded image can bring in hard-cash revenue. During the 1960s, when the West Coast main line was electrified from Euston to Manchester and Liverpool, the massive growth in patronage was termed the 'sparks effect'. This was defined as simply being the quantum leap in terms of image that electric trains brought about. The Southern Railway achieved much the same in the 1930s with its 'Southern Electric', and of course the legendary Frank Pick did it with his highly successful image for the London Underground.

But such equivalent 'sparks effects' for bus travel over the years have been far, far fewer. London Transport achieved a notable elevation of the image of semi-express bus travel in the 1930s with Green Line, and National Express made a worthy attempt with coach travel in the 1970s, although much of it was only paint and logos and the coach stations remained supremely awful.

There was also a very spirited effort to upgrade the perception of local bus travel in Stevenage between 1971 and 1980, with the 'Superbus' experiment, more particularly with the Metro-Scania single-deckers that were operated on the service. Surging uphill to Chells on a Scania certainly made bus travel feel as though someone somewhere was trying.

Then came deregulation, and in the early years the news wasn't all good. The industry moved to using breadvans with badgers or dolphins on their sides. Buses were suddenly in the news, but for all the wrong reasons — bus wars, bus jams, service failures, poor maintenance and, perhaps most visibly, their often 'cheap and cheerful' appearance. They certainly got the cheap bit right.

Of course, things improved, yet even as recently as the end of 2006 two associated operators — UK North and GM Buses — were removed from the streets of Manchester by the Traffic Commissioner after allegations of poor-quality training and maintenance.

Pizzazz

Meanwhile light rapid transit (LRT) has acquired an almost magical allure. The Tyne & Wear Metro opened in 1980, to be followed by the Docklands Light Railway (1987), Manchester Metrolink (1992), South Yorkshire Supertram (1994), Midland Metro (1999), Croydon Tramlink (2000) and Nottingham Express Transit (2004).

The image of travel on the earlier LRT systems was head and shoulders above bus travel, but Nottingham's in particular really seems to project the pizzazz that buses so desperately need if they are to capture the imagination of the young, the affluent and the impatient. You feel fashionable riding on the NET, you

don't on a Blogg's Buses Dennis Dart, well-designed though it is — or was.

Was. That is part of the problem. In many retail areas fashion changes rapidly. Look not just at clothes and shoes but at (say) mobile phones and computers. For a mobile-phone user, a three-year-old handset is a source of embarrassment, almost of shame. Five-year-old computers and televisions are virtually junk. And many people cannot bear to be seen owning a seven-or eight-year-old car. Yet we expect buses to last up to 20 years, and for consumers still to accept them as 'modern'. Twenty years in most consumers' minds is ancient.

Above: Light rail is seen in a positive light, although the reality isn't always quite as good as its supporters make out, as a bleak station and weed-infested track on the Manchester Metrolink show. Stewart J. Brown

Left: Do buses last too long? In service with Dunn-Line, a Volvo Citybus with East Lancs body arrives in Lincoln in 2006, at which time it was nearly 16 years old. And it looks old, when compared with the Stagecoach Wright Eclipse Gemini visible in the background. Stewart J. Brown

Aside from the vehicles themselves there's the issue of service reliability. The average citizen just isn't interested in operators' reasons for unreliability, the main bone of contention for bus users. Explanations for service failures are met with near-incredulity by passengers. Some passengers' comments have a stinging wit about them. "If I choose to ring them and complain, they will blame the weather. It's a bit windy today, yes … It's unfortunate — wind has a detrimental effect on bus engines, causing them to demagnetise and slowly fall to pieces … It's also raining … Rain will cause a bus driver to curl into the fœtal position at the mere sight of the phenomenon …"

Some areas have even held competitions for the worst bus service. During 2006 the competition in Portsmouth produced a shortlist of five routes, the winner being the No 14. Passengers in Norfolk voted their service from Wymondham to Norwich as the worst around, adding that their complaints went unanswered.

Continuing decline?

Whether due to operator shortcomings, design deficiencies or other, more fundamental reasons, such as rising income or the importing from the USA of 'prairie planning', with its out-of-town retail parks and business parks, or just the fact that most people want cars and then use them for every single imaginable journey purpose, it's hard to quantify. The grim fact is that bus use has sagged very badly outside London

over the past decade or two, especially in the major cities, where buses should be a vital tool of any progressive transport policy.

For example, between 1996 and 2006, bus use across the five English Passenger Transport Executive areas fell by a startling 18%, or almost one fifth. That equates to about 14 permanently vacated seats on every formerly full double-decker. If that rate of decline were maintained *ad absurdum* bus travel in the large metropolitan cities outside London would hit the nil axis and completely disappear within most of our lifetimes. Those hypothetical double-deckers would be empty.

The calls for improving the image of bus travel have thus recently become louder and yet louder still.

A fresh image

All this adds up to a situation that is, to use the current popular term, challenging. So what can be done? There are now some real signs that the bus industry in the UK is trying hard to leave the 20th century — and that difficult marketing image of the past two or three decades — behind.

It's not just that the Atlanteans, Fleetlines, Nationals, Bristols and, of course, the much-loved and iconic Routemasters have now finally gone from ordinary

Below: Across the PTE areas as a whole bus use dropped by 18% between 1996 and 2006. This is Merseyside, with an Arriva Dennis Dart/Marshall and Volvo B10B/Wright. Stewart J. Brown

Left: The sublime and the ridiculous? First's innovative StreetCar passes a 22-year-old Leyland Olympian in York in 2006. The reality of bus travel includes dramatic differences in vehicle quality. Stewart J. Brown

Right: Thanks to massive public funding London's bus fleet is 100% low-floor and has an average age of just five years. Investment in new vehicles, staff training and the introduction of new routes have all helped contribute to a rise in bus use in the capital. So too has the congestion charge. Stewart J. Brown

Left: Outside London the average age of Britain's buses is eight years — represented by an eight-year-old Dennis Trident with First Glasgow. This vehicle started life in London and was displaced by newer vehicles in 2005. Do Glasgow bus users know that they're travelling on an old London bus? Does it matter, as long as it's clean, and the service is reliable? Stewart J. Brown

service. In 2006 FirstGroup commenced operation of its 'ftr' articulated buses in York. These colourful serpents have tried hard superficially to resemble LRT cars, and, although there were some significant teething troubles with aspects of the service, it was at long last a commendably bold attempt to redefine what buses should look like, and what bus travel should feel like. Maybe only 7 out of 10 for actual results this time around, but undoubtedly full marks for trying.

Buses have been getting younger too, on average, now that the classics of the past have moved on to that Great Bus Garage in the Sky (Barnsley, to be more prosaic) or to rally fields. By mid-2006 the average age of local buses in Britain was just over eight years. In London it was under five years, the lowest it had probably been since the completion of the mass introduction of RTs and RFs in the early 1950s.

There have also been improvements in assisting personal security. Across the whole of Britain, by 2006 nearly 40% of local buses had CCTV, while in London the figure recently reached 90%. Not everyone welcomes this, but it does give some reassurance to vulnerable passengers.

Where next? Perhaps we should go back to the late Barbara Castle's New Bus Grant, whereby operators received a major subsidy for equipping their fleets with new kit. It might sound politically retro, but any such scheme would be much more simple to implement and could bring about a really rapid improvement in emissions, as well as completing the low-floor revolution. Grants could also kick-start innovative

propulsion schemes — we'd better give the chicken-manure-powered systems a miss, but there are plenty of promising technologies to have a go at — and could get guided-bus or trolleybus proposals moving where these showed genuine promise. When you compare the subsidies paid to rail operators with those paid for improving bus travel, the contrast is a startling one.

If the image of the bus can be turned round, and if it can be booted forward, well into the 21st century, leaving the 1980s and 1990s behind for ever, and if it can start to look like a modern transit system rather than a basement-level form of transport for children and older people, then the bus has a bright future. It has so much going for it — full car parks, higher motoring taxes, the stress of driving, growing public alarm over climate change, and a realisation that we can't go on living the way we are living at the moment — that it just has to succeed.

But the industry, and Government, must face up to bus travel's faults and candidly confront its demons. And, who knows, we might just turn significant numbers of today's non-users into users. And perhaps even convert a few into enthusiasts …

Below: Modern vehicles, attractive liveries, partnerships with local authorities, real-time information, improved service frequencies — all help make bus travel more attractive. In 2006 Preston Bus adopted a new image with the introduction of its first Scanias, which replaced Leyland Lynxes. They had East Lancs' new Esteem body. Stewart J. Brown

Ten years of low-floor 'deckers

The first low-floor double-decker entered service in Bristol 10 years ago. **STEWART J. BROWN** looks at developments in what has been a rapidly changing market.

Above: **The old order. Among the last step-entrance double-deckers — and the last for London — was this Volvo Olympian with Northern Counties body, seen at the Alperton depot of First's CentreWest business before entering service in the spring of 1999. It carries short-lived First Challenger fleetnames.** Stewart J. Brown

The move to low-floor models has brought about one of the fastest changes in the history of double-deck bus operation in Britain. The first low-floor double-decker, a DAF DB250, entered service in February 1998 with ABus of Bristol. Just over two-and-a-half years later the last of the previous generation of what became known as step-entrance

double-deckers were being delivered. The very last was an East Lancs-bodied Scania N113 which entered service with Hardings of Liverpool towards the end of 2000. It was the last of a batch of 30 built for stock and which were bought by a variety of small operators during the year.

Consider the last big change in double-deck design, the introduction of the rear-engined Leyland Atlantean. The first production Atlantean entered service with Wallasey Corporation in 1958, but it was fully 11 years later that the last front-engined half-cab took to Britain's streets — a Leyland Titan PD3 ordered by Ramsbottom Urban District Council and delivered to the newly created South East Lancashire North East Cheshire Passenger Transport Executive.

The move away from half-cabs would probably have taken even longer were it not for the Government's New Bus Grant scheme, which was introduced in 1968 to speed the adoption of one-man operation by encouraging operators to buy suitable designs of bus. This encouragement took the form of a 25% grant towards the purchase price — but only for buses of an appropriate specification. That excluded half-cabs.

The much speedier adoption of low-floor models four decades later was driven by pressure from groups representing disabled people and by legislation setting out a timetable which insisted on the purchase of accessible buses for use on scheduled services — and which will eventually see non-accessible buses being prohibited.

The best-selling model in the final days of the old regime was the Volvo Olympian. The original Olympian had been launched by Leyland back in 1980, and had been progressively updated by both Leyland and Volvo over the years.

But while Volvo may have dominated double-deck sales in the 1990s it was Dennis that would lead the way in low-floor double-deckers, much as it had with low-floor single-deckers. Its first entered service not in Britain but in Hong Kong — with the Kowloon Motor Bus Co, in September 1997. Dennis was an established supplier of double-deck buses to Hong Kong, first with the front-engined Jubilant, then with the two-axle Dominator, followed by the three-axle Condor and Dragon. So the introduction of the three-axle low-floor Trident was a logical progression.

But in Britain the picture for Dennis was rather different. The Dominator's last good year in Britain was 1991, when just under 50 entered service. After that Dominator sales plummeted — eight in 1992, three in 1993 and then a final four in 1996. That's just 15 Dennis double-deckers for UK operators in a five-year period. The lighter Arrow model, based on the single-deck Lance, did boost Dennis double-deck sales from 1996 to 1998 but was hardly a mainstream model, with just two significant customers, London & Country and Capital Citybus. But that was about to change.

The 1997 Coach & Bus show was the launch pad for the low-floor double-decker. DAF had in fact showed a suitable chassis at the 1995 show, but it was 1997 before a complete vehicle appeared, and this had an Optare Spectra body. The vehicle used to launch the new low-floor Spectra — which looked little different from the original step-entrance model — was one of two for the National Express Group. The first entered service with Travel West Midlands in February 1998, followed soon after by the second, which went to Travel Dundee and was Scotland's first low-floor double-decker.

At the 1997 show Dennis exhibited a Hong Kong three-axle Trident, with Alexander ALX500 bodywork, and also announced its biggest-ever British double-deck bus order: 100 two-axle Tridents for Stagecoach. This was a remarkable coup for Dennis, for although it

had supplied Darts and Javelins to Stagecoach the Scottish-based group was firmly wedded to Volvo when it came to buying double-deckers. Or so, at least, it had seemed.

In developing its low-floor model Volvo scored a spectacular own goal. It tried to convince British operators that the bus they wanted was the B7L, a model designed for use as a single-decker in Continental Europe. This had a side-mounted engine in the rear overhang (anyone remember the Bristol VRL?) and it was manifestly unsuited for the British market as a double-decker (and, as Volvo would find out to its cost, was not really that acceptable as a single-decker either). Ironically, it was a B7L which was the star of the 1997 show, but that was because it was the first showing of Plaxton's stylish new President body, built at the former Northern Counties factory in Wigan.

Inside and out, the President was stunning. It eclipsed Optare's Spectra — which had in its time been the model against which others were judged — and outshone Alexander's ALX500. At the show Volvo kept an almost embarrassed silence, saying as little as it could about its new chassis while Dennis, which had not yet built a two-axle Trident, was trumpeting its success with Stagecoach. And it was a remarkable

Below: **Britain's first modern low-floor double-decker was this DAF DB250/Optare Spectra, which entered service in Bristol with ABus in February 1998.** Andrew Jarosz

success, with Stagecoach going on to standardise on the Trident at Volvo's expense.

While the new DAF was launched with an Optare body, other choices were available. DAF's first major order for its low-floor chassis came from the Cowie Group, which announced it was taking 63 with Alexander ALX400 bodywork for operation in London.

The ill-fated Volvo B7L did do some demonstration work on trade plates but was never registered for service — and, although it could be driven, it was moved between demonstration venues on a low-loader. Volvo's designers headed rapidly back to their drawing boards or, more accurately, to their computer monitors.

As mentioned above, it was DAF that was first to get low-floor double-deckers onto Britain's streets, with vehicles for ABus and National Express Group in 1998. Further DAFs followed during the year, most notably for Arriva, as the Cowie Group had by then become. These heralded London's low-floor double-deck revolution, and while they certainly made for easier access they were not without their critics. The main complaint was a lack of seats downstairs. The buses were easy to board, but once you were on board there were not many accessible seats.

Although no Dennis double-deckers were delivered in 1998 the company was busy taking orders from operators that had previously bought Volvo Olympians — First CentreWest ordered 31, Lothian Region Transport 10, and Metroline 91. Lothian, which had been buying Alexander-bodied Olympians, switched to Plaxton-bodied Tridents and by 2000 had almost 100 in service. It would ultimately be running almost 200.

Volvo, meanwhile, struggling to recover lost ground, announced in August that it would be offering a revised chassis, the B7TL, with a transverse engine. Operators could be excused for responding: "We told you so!" But it did secure orders — 91 for London Central and London General, and six for Lothian. These would be Lothian's last Volvo double-deckers until the collapse of TransBus undermined the position of the Trident and Lothian reverted to Volvo as its main supplier. Travel West Midlands soon joined the list of Volvo buyers, with an initial order for 102. More would follow, not just for the West Midlands but for TWM's associated operations in Dundee and London.

East Lancs got ready to join the bodybuilders offering new designs on low-floor double-deckers with the development of its ADD99 (Aluminium Double Decker 1999) model. This was announced at the end of 1998 as the Lolyne, and the first order, for 12, was placed by Nottingham City Transport. ADD99 developed into a family of outwardly similar bodies. The Lolyne was built on the Trident, the Vyking on the B7TL, and the Myllennium on the DB250. The Myllennium featured a different style of front, which was then made available on the Lolyne and Vyking too.

The year of big change in London was 1999. When the year started there were around two dozen low-floor double-deckers in the capital — all Alexander-bodied DAFs with Arriva. By the end of the year there were more than 600, most of them Dennises running for Blue Triangle, First, Metrobus, Metroline and Stagecoach. There were also more DAFs for Arriva and a few for the short-lived Capital Logistics company.

London's last step-entrance double-deckers were 20 Volvo Olympians with Northern Counties Palatine I bodies, which entered service in the spring of 1999. They shared a T-KLF registration series with Dennis Tridents.

Dennis supplied more than 600 Tridents to UK fleets in 1999, which was a remarkable performance for the company. Its best-ever performance with the old Dominator in the UK — way back in 1982 — had been just 159 sales, a figure of which Dennis was no doubt proud at the time. However, this was the year in which Volvo started its comeback. Having announced the B7TL in August 1998, it unveiled the first example of its new model 12 months later. Deliveries started in 2000.

The big event in bus manufacturing in 2000 was the creation of TransBus, formed by a merger of Mayflower's Dennis and Alexander businesses with Henlys' Plaxton. This was to prove a turning point for all concerned, although not in the way they intended. There was over-capacity at TransBus's body plants, and this the new company failed to address. Ultimately — in 2004 — the business collapsed, and this gave Volvo the opportunity it needed to build on growing B7TL sales and regain its position as the leading supplier of double-deck buses to UK operators.

Although the key component parts of the TransBus bus-building business would survive in the new Alexander Dennis company the collapse of TransBus undermined many operators' confidence in the Trident. A new model from Alexander Dennis, the Enviro400, saw the start of a recovery in double-deck sales. It was launched in 2005, and soon secured orders from Metroline, Go-Ahead (in London) and Stagecoach. At Stagecoach it has succeeded the Dennis Trident with Alexander ALX400 body as the group's standard double-decker.

By integrating the design of the Guildford-built chassis with the Falkirk-built body Alexander Dennis maximised the number of seats available on the lower deck. The Enviro400 body has also been built on Volvo chassis, while the Dennis-built chassis is available to other bodybuilders, the first taker being East Lancs.

The Enviro400 replaced both the ALX400 and the President. The Wigan factory which built the President was closed in 2005.

In the meantime Scania, which had been absent

Above: The original style of East Lancs bodywork for low-floor chassis, seen here in service with Mayne of Manchester. This is a Lolyne body on a Dennis Trident. Stewart J. Brown

Below: A VDL DB250 with East Lancs body operated by TM Travel of Chesterfield. The unusually shaped upper-deck windscreen was a feature of Myllennium-style bodies from East Lancs. Gavin Booth

Top: The Oxford Bus Company was an early buyer of the Dennis Trident with Alexander ALX400 bodywork, taking 20 in 1999. They were dual-door 71-seaters. This one is seen on one of the city's park-and-ride services in 2006. Gavin Booth

Above: The Alexander ALX400 body continued largely unchanged under TransBus ownership — only the oval badge under the fleetname identifies this First London Volvo B7TL as a TransBus rather than an Alexander body. The ALX400 was built at two locations — Falkirk and Belfast. Peter Rowlands

Above: The stylish Plaxton President on Dennis Trident chassis was selected by Lothian Buses as its standard double-decker after many years of buying Alexander-bodied Olympians. A few were specified as coaches for operation to Edinburgh Airport. Gavin Booth

Below: The Plaxton President, built at the former Northern Counties factory in Wigan, was a striking design. Metroline was one of the first users and also got the last of the type. This is a 2004 Volvo B7TL. Stewart J. Brown

from the double-deck business since selling its last N113s in 2000, made a reappearance in 2002 with its N94UD, initially available only with East Lancs OmniDekka bodywork. The biggest buyer of Scania low-floor double-deckers has been Go-Ahead, primarily for its Metrobus and Brighton & Hove fleets. The OmniDekka uses a standard Scania-style front panel, linking it visually with Scania's complete Polish-built OmniCity range.

In 2001 a new name — Wright of Ballymena — appeared in double-deck bodies. Wright had in the previous decade become a substantial builder of stylish single-deck buses, and it brought its design flair to the double-deck market with the striking Eclipse Gemini on the Volvo B7TL. The first were for Arriva London (which later added Pulsar Geminis on DAF chassis). The Gemini name was a play on the zodiac sign for twins — for a twin-deck bus.

The eye-catching Gemini quickly won new customers for Wright, generally at the expense of the Alexander business in Falkirk. In London Geminis were bought in large numbers by Go-Ahead, First, Arriva, Travel London and East Thames Buses. Elsewhere significant buyers included Lothian Buses, First and Travel West Midlands. Blazefield opted for the Eclipse Gemini for a luxurious fleet of double-deckers used to raise quality standards on its service between Harrogate and Leeds; later the group introduced Geminis to its Yorkshire Coastliner and Burnley & Pendle businesses.

As Wright expanded one established bodybuilder withdrew from double-deck production. Since 1991 Optare had been building its attractive Spectra on DAF

(latterly VDL) chassis. The last Spectra entered service in 2006. The company had for some time been promising a revolutionary new model, which was expected to have a side-mounted engine — a layout last seen in Britain 70 years ago on the AEC Q. But uncertainty over long-term production volumes and the fact that Optare missed out on the rapid updating of London's double-deck fleet in the early 2000s — meaning there will be a lull before sizeable orders come again from the capital — saw the project put to one side. Instead Optare concentrated on developing products for which it could see more immediate sales potential. Not that the Optare project is dead — just dormant.

Volvo's original B7L in double-deck form did, in the end, find two UK customers. In 2002 First Glasgow took 10, with East Lancs bodywork, generally similar to vehicles being supplied to Denmark. These were 12m-long three-axle air-conditioned 95-seaters, with a total capacity of 115. And in 2005 Arriva took a batch with stylish open-top Ayats bodies to introduce accessible buses to its London sightseeing tour. These, incidentally, were later joined by open-top conversions of Plaxton Presidents, on DAF chassis, which had been displaced from the Arriva London bus fleet.

In 2004 Scania announced that it would be building a complete CN94UD OmniCity double-decker at its Polish factory, thereby ending the exclusive relationship

Above: Scania's low-floor double-decker was initially available only with East Lancs' OmniDekka body. This example, operated by Greater Manchester independent Bullock, features high-backed seats. Stewart J. Brown

Below: Following the collapse of TransBus Lothian Buses switched to Volvo B7TL chassis with Wright bodywork. Stewart J. Brown

Above: The Wright Gemini is surely the most striking double-deck design on Britain's streets. Arriva London was the first user of the type and runs Eclipse Geminis on Volvo B7TL chassis and Pulsar Geminis on VDL DB250s. Two VDLs lay over at Oxford Circus. Stewart J. Brown

Below: The Wright Eclipse Gemini is widely used by First in its fleets around the country. This example was delivered to First Glasgow in 2004. Stewart J. Brown

Above: First does operate small numbers of other types of low-floor double-decker in its fleets outside London, including East Lancs-bodied Scanias at First Edinburgh. Gavin Booth

Below: The B7L is a rare beast in double-deck form, operating in the UK only with First Glasgow and, as here, with Arriva on its London sightseeing tour. Ayats built the attractive body. Stewart J. Brown

that had seen all Scania double-deckers bodied by East Lancs. The first production vehicles were delivered to Lothian Buses in the summer of 2006, followed soon after by vehicles for Transdev's London United business. In 2007 Travel West Midlands also placed orders for complete Scania double-deckers, having had one of the prototypes in service since 2005.

East Lancs has long had a positive attitude to chassis manufacturers looking for a partner. So when MAN decided to start selling double-deckers in the UK it was East Lancs that provided the bodywork, launching the new MAN model at the 2006 Euro Bus exhibition in Birmingham with an unusual 4m-high example. Building an urban bus to such a low height meant restricted headroom inside, but it showed what could be done. Production vehicles will be built to more generous dimensions.

The MAN/East Lancs double-decker, the Kinetic, uses a standard MAN front panel and windscreen, which sets it apart from other East Lancs models. The Kinetic is a variant of a new East Lancs double-deck body, the Olympus, which was unveiled in 2006. This is offered on chassis from Alexander Dennis, Scania, VDL and Volvo. It replaces the previous double-deck range, of which more than 1,000 were built, although the OmniDekka remains available on

Scania chassis. The first Olympus, on a Volvo B9TL, was for Delaine of Bourne.

To meet new exhaust-emissions legislation which came into force in 2006 Volvo replaced its B7TL with the new B9TL, which uses a bigger, 9-litre engine in place of the 7.3-litre unit of the previous model. The B9TL is also available with three axles and in this configuration has been bodied by Wrightbus for KMB in Hong Kong, by Alexander Dennis for Dublin Bus and by East Lancs for a very small number of UK fleets.

Scania also changed engines at Euro 4, switching from a six-cylinder to a five-cylinder unit, still of 9-litre capacity. Its double-deck model nomenclature changed as well. Out went the N94 ('9' indicating the 9-litre engine, '4' the 4-series chassis) and in its place came the N270 (the engine power output, measured in bhp).

The Dennis Trident had been powered by the 8.3-litre Cummins ISCe engine, and that was fitted to early Enviro400s, but for Euro 4 Alexander Dennis switched to the smaller Cummins ISBe 6.7-litre engine. When launched the Enviro400 was also advertised as being available with a 7.2-litre Caterpillar engine but this option quietly vanished in 2006.

Below: **In 2006 complete Polish-built Scania OmniCity double-deckers were ordered by two fleets — Transdev and Lothian Buses. Transdev took 15.** Stewart J. Brown

The double-deck bus in Britain has had a more chequered career than many might realise. In the mid-1960s the popularity of one-man-operated standee single-deckers raised questions about the double-decker's future. That popularity was short-lived (and, in fairness was never shared by bus users, only by a small number of bus operators), and the double-decker bounced back.

Then, 20 years later, the rush to buy minibuses and cut costs saw double-deck production plummet, and this impacted on such big-name suppliers as ECW, MCW and even the mighty Leyland.

Changes in London from the late 1980s saw first minibuses and then midibuses being used to replace double-deckers in large numbers, the Dennis Dart being the most common choice for London fleets. But that changed too, as the focus moved to combining

Above: **The first MAN double-deck bus for operation in Britain was unveiled at the 2006 Euro Bus Expo event at the National Exhibition Centre. It was built to a height of just 4m — production models will be higher — and entered service with Reading Buses in 2007.** Stewart J. Brown

high service frequencies with high passenger capacity to revolutionise London's bus system. Artics offered the highest carrying capacity, but double-deckers were the chosen vehicle for most services.

And there have been concerns over vehicle choice. Thirty years ago Leyland had a virtual monopoly of the double-deck market. Now there are five chassis manufacturers and a choice of four bodybuilders.

The demise of the double-decker has long been predicted, but, if history is any guide, it will be around for a long time yet.

The double-deck choice, 2008

	Body	Alexander Dennis	East Lancs	Scania	Wrightbus
Chassis					
Alexander Dennis		x	x		
MAN			x		
Scania			x	x	
VDL Bus			x		x
Volvo		x	x		x

Glasgow's 21st-century independents

Although three of the UK's biggest transport groups dominate Glasgow's bus services, there have been a number of smaller operators serving the city. **BILLY NICOL** illustrates a selection of those that have been running since 2000.

Left: In 2001 the short-lived Dart Buses, based in Paisley, entered an agreement with Stagecoach which saw some Dart vehicles running in Stagecoach livery. These included this Marshall-bodied MAN 11.220, which had been bought new by Dart in 1999.

Left: It's not only First that operates artics in Glasgow. This Wright-bodied Scania L94UA is used by Doigs, primarily on a contracted service for the University of Strathclyde. The 'olde worlde' lettering used for Doig's fleetname contrasts with the modern lines of the Solar Eclipse Fusion body.

Left: In addition to its Lanarkshire services McKindless has a significant presence in Glasgow and has operated several routes which have competed with First. Unusual vehicles in the fleet were low-floor Berkhof-bodied Dennis Lances, which started out as airport transfer buses at Heathrow. One is seen on the approach to Buchanan Bus Station, followed by a First Glasgow Leyland Tiger.

Right: Caledonia Buses started operating in 2002, competing with First on services running south from the city centre. A varied fleet of second-hand vehicles has been used, including this former Metroline MAN 11.220 with Marshall body, seen loading in Union Street on the company's service to Clarkston.

Left: Dickson of Paisley has been operating on the Glasgow-Paisley corridor since 1992. Mercedes-Benz minibuses have been the dominant type in the fleet, but there have also been Dennis Dart SLFs with Plaxton Pointer bodywork, which were new to Armchair of London.

Right: Not to be confused with First is First Stop Travel, which runs a network of services in south-west Glasgow. A former Plymouth CityBus Plaxton-bodied Mercedes-Benz 709D is seen in Govan on the company's Paisley service.

Left: Puma commenced operation of a service between Govan Cross and Pollock in 1992, launching it in competition with Strathclyde Buses. The service still operates. Among the vehicles used has been this early Dennis Dart with Carlyle body.

Right: Glasgow Citybus was formed in 1999, operating in the north-west of the city and out to Clydebank. Its fleet has included this DAF SB220 with Optare Delta body. The business was purchased by West Coast Motors at the start of 2006.

Left: Many of Glasgow's small operators have chosen to run minibuses, including City Sprinter, which was established in 1997 and competes with First Glasgow on a service from the city centre to Eastwood Toll. This Mercedes-Benz 709D was new to Thames Transit.